#1 INTERNATIONAL BESTSELLER

PARAMORPHING

The Secret Ancient Priesthood Science of Effortlessly Transforming Physical Reality and Obtaining All Dreams and Desires

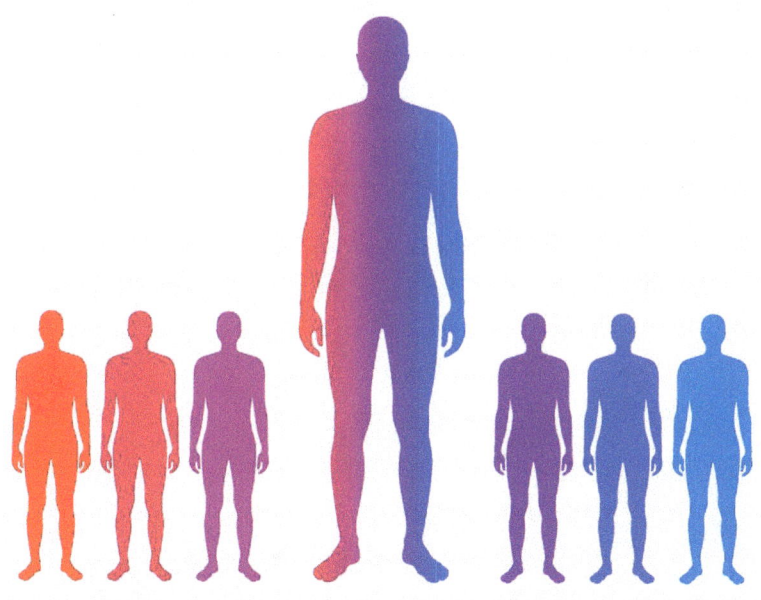

HARI R. MIRA

Copyright © 2024 Hari Mira
All rights reserved.
No portion of this book may be reproduced in any form without written permission from the publisher or author except as permitted by U.S. copyright law.

Table Of Contents

Chapter 1: Introduction 1

Chapter 2: Defining Paramorphing 8

Chapter 3: The Core Paramorphing Process 18

Chapter 4: Master Beliefs and Heart Harmony 36

   The 3 Paramorphing Master Beliefs 36

   The Heart's Harmonic Signature 39

Chapter 5: The 7 Flavors of Friction 43

   Factor 1: Doubt and Delusion 43

   Factor 2: Pedestalization of the Desired PRL 55

   Factor 3: Aversion to the Existing PRL 2 58

   Factor 4: Extreme Seriousness 62

   Factor 5: Insufficient Surrender 66

   Factor 6: Lack of True Desire 71

   Factor 7: Habituation to the Past 76

Chapter 6: The Practical Application of Paramorphing 81

   The Inside-Out Method 83

      Embodying Desired PRLs 83

      Disembodying Undesired PRLs 94

   The Outside-In Method 98

      The Encyclopedia Technique 98

      The Reality Draping Technique 101

      The Confirmation Benefit Technique 107

      The 7 Magical Paramorphing Mantras 115

Chapter 7: Questions and Answers 116

Dedication

God, the Infinite and Omnipotent Creator of Love and Light

Humanity, the Beloved Sons and Daughters of God

My Beloved Pleiadean Family

All Saints, Prophets, Mystics, Visionaries, and Teachers of God

Chapter 1: Introduction

Paramorphing is the language and process that God, the Supreme Creator, uses to conceive, create, modify, and reshape the physical universe. Anyone who has ever achieved anything in any domain has used Paramorphing, whether they are conscious of it or not. **Paramorphing is the supreme divine law of the universe that transcends and comes before all other laws.**

Most people barely know the language and accordingly, only make limited progress toward obtaining their heart's desires. They do not realize that they can truly have anything they dream of. Those who speak Paramorphing fluently, on the other hand, can shape their reality exactly as they choose. They have learned to speak God's language, so they start creating like God: Powerfully, predictably, efficiently, and with unwavering conviction. This book will teach you how to speak God's secret language.

My name is Hari. I grew up in the United States and have a background in psychological research, spiritual studies, applied metacognition, and allegorical religion. "Before" my present birth on planet Earth, I was an inhabitant of a much lighter, sweeter, gentler, and immensely more beautiful astral realm which I consider to be my true home. I use "before" with quotation marks for time is a construct I am subject to while I am on Earth; in reality, however, all my lives and all your lives are happening RIGHT NOW (we will discuss this later). I am not the first such being to come to Earth. Through the history of this planet, countless beings from other realms have come to Earth. Humans worship a few of them as Gods, but they never intended to be Gods: They came here to remind you that you are just as worthy as them and equally divine children of the Creator. We are not superior to humans, nor do we judge humans. In fact, we admire and salute humans for their resilience while functioning on a planet that has such a high degree of adversity, negativity, and hardship. We are simply here to awaken humans to their true potential as infinite embodiments of God, capable of doing, being, or having absolutely anything.

In any case, I came here to help the planet in her spiritual ascension toward becoming Heaven on Earth, rather than the Earth we see presently. I can offer no proof for any of these claims. I simply know that what I say is the truth and those who are ready will benefit immensely from this small but potent book. The simple fact that this book has found its way into your hands is a fairly robust indicator that you will understand, value, and implement the life-changing advice here to make all your dreams and desires come true. Yes, it is possible. And more importantly, YOU are ready to finally hear the truth of how to consciously take control of your entire life. I am not superior to you in any way, for underneath superficial differences we are the same deep down: Rays of the Creator, children of the One God, imbued with infinite power.

Paramorphing is the gift that God, the creator, has given us all, so it belongs to you as much as it belongs to me. Your soul knows everything in this book; you've merely temporarily forgotten it, and I'm merely reminding you of the latent powers that are hidden within you. It is time to wake up and assert your inner glory.

Paramorphing is the culmination of all spiritual wisdom and does not require any prior background knowledge. It is comprehensive and flawlessly reliable because the divine laws of creation are unfailing, absolute, and eternal. Modern scientific frameworks such as quantum physics have started to slowly grasp specks of these great truths, but it will be a while before humanity on Earth advances to fully cognize how creation actually works. The good news is you don't need to know all the nuts and bolts. In the same way that you can operate a laptop without knowing the intricacies of how a circuit board comes together, you can apply the principles contained in this book to get anything you desire in life. Yes, anything means ANYTHING.

If you are a spiritually sensitive soul or someone who feels that things are not "quite right" on Earth, Paramorphing will allow you to rapidly move from feeling stuck, miserable, and confused to discovering the master key that allows you to control every atom of your existence, from reversing health struggles to getting people to treat you differently to enjoying material abundance in spades. However, all of these are merely secondary side effects or shadows of learning the greatest truth contained in this work: That you are God and the sole master, architect, and scriptwriter of your physical reality.

Paramorphing has been closely guarded by secret and (usually) reclusive organizations around the world. Emperors, pharaohs, religious heads, priests, princes, moguls, kings, and tzars were carefully instructed in these truths, irrespective of where they were in the world. On the surface level, they had different rules, laws, and norms that they established for their societies, but above all, the fundamental and sacred truths that they believed, lived by, and guarded were ONE. From Mesopotamia to Giza, from Babylon to Rome, and from the Indus Valley to Athens, the different ancient secret texts, scriptures, and occult doctrines guarded by these groups ALL boil down to the fundamental truths of creation contained in this work. My forefathers were bearers of this truth and belonged to one such priesthood group. I suppose I was born into such a family in order to aid the work and mission I came to Earth for, but I do not know for sure. Nonetheless, my mission is clear: To share the foundational principles of Paramorphing with the world.

Yes, this is a short work. Why? Because the truth is simple, succinct, and experiential. God, formless and eternal, descends into the world of form and becomes limited objects and creatures to enjoy his own eternal infinitude by experiencing himself in countless ways, knowing that he can never truly be harmed. **This is the holy grail.** If you can fully grasp, live, and embody this, you do not really need to learn anything else, or even read the rest of this book.

There is no need to spend years reading massive, dusty tomes in secret libraries to unveil the holy grail. The greatest things in the world are perfectly simple and humble, and because God is the grandest phenomenon of them all, he is the epitome of simplicity and humility. In fact, Paramorphing is so obvious, so simple, and so succinct that it can seem too good or too easy to be true. Paramorphing doesn't require a book. It can be summarized in a sentence or two. I've only written a book because the veil of amnesia on Earth is so strong that the vast majority of humans assume themselves to be limited and powerless, not realizing that they have the infinite power, love, wisdom, joy, and glory of God coursing through them each and every second.

The core rules of creation are incredibly simple. The "catch", if you will, is not in the law of Paramorphing itself, which is pristinely pure and unbelievably simple, but in applying it effectively. The astute reader who intuitively realizes the priceless value of this work will immediately stop asking questions, test the teachings by putting them into practice, adapt and experiment, and reap the rewards through direct experience. No amount of theoretical speculation can replace the joy, power, and conviction you will feel when you actually start transforming the world around you.

God, or Source, is an honest and untrickable phenomenon. It simply, clearly, and faithfully reproduces and creates whatever you are truly conscious of being. It does not care for or reward uncertainty, speculation, doubt, excitement, fear, cleverness, craving, or holier-than-thou posturing. God rewards assertive decisiveness, honesty, and detached firmness in claiming a particular outcome without searching for proof among the world of the senses and "facts" (which do not exist in reality, as you will learn shortly, for everything that you perceive is your own creation).

Could you put a price on reversing a cancer diagnosis? Going from broke to receiving money effortlessly? Instantly repairing a strained relationship with a loved one? No amount of money, I reiterate, could match the value of what you hold in your hands (or on your screen) right now. I have witnessed fatal tumors disappear overnight. I have seen massive debts mysteriously vanish. I have seen people chased, loved, and devotedly pursued by relatives and romantic partners who despised them just months ago. I have witnessed people overcoming unthinkable odds by receiving gifts, surprises, and miracles that no amount of rational linear thinking could possibly explain. Paramorphing is the astral science of invoking the infinite power of your higher Self, which is yoked to God. And with God, all things are truly possible, far beyond "rationality". In fact, to assume that miracles are not possible is just about the least "rational" belief out there.

Once you internalize Paramorphing, it is my humble recommendation that you stay quiet about creating your reality instead of foisting your new knowledge and powers upon those around you. Of course, this is merely a recommendation, and you are welcome to totally disregard anything I say in this book if you wish, but I have my reasons for saying what I say. Quietly use these priceless principles to get whatever you want in the world without trying to show off your newfound wisdom, unless you feel you have a deep inner calling and spiritual directive or mission to teach others. **It is also recommended that you do not share your copy of this work with anyone else. It is your charmed keepsake and a personal amulet.** You may encourage someone to buy a copy of this book if you would like but do not provide any further details or compel or persuade them to purchase it. Those who are meant to find it will; those who are not will find it at a "later" date. And that is perfectly fine. Everything ultimately works out perfectly, just as it should.

Your primary focus should be on creating your world in whatever way you desire. You will awaken your divine capability to do exactly this after reading this book and internalizing it.

You may wonder how Paramorphing is similar to or different from concepts that are popular on earth at this time such as reality creation, manifestation, the law of attraction, non-duality, and others. The truth is that Paramorphing not only agrees with all these in the deepest way but takes them many steps further by offering a practical guide to actually create change in one's physical circumstances. Many traditions often promote ideas such as "you become what you think" or simply "ask and then receive". These teachings are true, but have you had results from them? Or do they honestly sound like new-age hogwash? Perhaps you've been able to manifest "small" things such as a little gift, a free cup of coffee, or a friendly chat from someone who used to resent you. But what about the "big" things like reversing major health challenges, securing financial independence, solving seemingly unfixable problems in unexpectedly miraculous ways, finding lasting love, breaking records in your chosen field, or even visiting other realms (yes, they exist, as we will discuss shortly)? Why do the law of attraction, the law of resonance, the law of vibration, and the other laws of creation appear to behave "unpredictably" or "only for the small things"? In truth, there is nothing "big" or "small" in God's eyes of perfect equality, but it is only YOU that needs to change in order to transform any area of your life. And you can.

Yes, that is correct: There is nothing "external" that you need to control or hope for. You can change anything in your external perceived reality by changing your imaginative self-concept. You have total control, though the illusion of being a human on Earth often makes you forget this truth.

Paramorphing is the king of kings, the law of laws, the system of all systems. It is the very foundation of the universe itself. Once you learn Paramorphing, you will understand the limitations, challenges, and pitfalls of other laws. You will see why you have successfully created the things you wished for in certain areas of your life while also realizing why other areas haven't panned out as you may have desired (and how to reverse that going forward).

Paramorphing, in short, is the language God uses to conceive, create, and reshape the world.

Now you, as a son or daughter of God, will learn how to speak the most useful, most powerful, and most versatile language in the world to start shaping your reality just like God does.

Over the course of this book, I will draw on references from various religious and spiritual texts. This is not because I necessarily recommend or espouse any particular religion, but because the truths of Paramorphing are nestled within every great spiritual work. The teachings of the greatest spiritual teachers throughout history have been altered via human error or even sheer malice to keep divine truths out of the hands of the common person. The priest class throughout history has veiled, obscured, or outright modified the truths of Paramorphing to control the masses and prevent them from realizing their true potential as sons and daughters of God, the Supreme Creator. However, the great spiritual works written by spiritual luminaries still contain many kernels and nuggets of Paramorphing wisdom. Recognizing and meditating on these words will help you internalize Paramorphing to create your dream life.

Let us now begin.

* * * * * * * * *

Chapter 2: Defining Paramorphing

Paramorphing is the language and process God, the Supreme Creator, uses to create and experience physical reality.

God is pure, formless, limitless, and indestructible creative energy. God is ALL THAT IS, the whole, utterly indivisible, and beyond judgments, limitations, or labels.

God simply is. The nature of God is eternal existence or "isness".

God is often described as vast stillness or the peace that passes all understanding, and this is true. However, it is not because God is unmoving. It is because God's creative energy is pure love, and love has such an infinitely high frequency that it appears to be still. The infinitely subtle, powerful, and loving creative energy of God seeks to express itself in an infinite number of ways. However, God's latent state is one of wholeness and utter completeness, being all that is.

This creates a paradox: If God is all that is, how can this infinitely powerful creative energy create anything or experience anything? Suppose a group of people lived on a planet where the sun shone brightly for 24 hours each day, without a break, perpetually. From birth, they have only seen perpetually sunny skies, with no concept of day or night, for they look identical. If you were to tell these people about the joys of a starry night, or the pleasures of a purple-orange twilight, or the melancholy moods of a grey-cloudy sky, they would simply not understand you. If you have only seen sunny skies for your entire life, it becomes impossible to fathom an overcast sky or the concept of day and night.

God, the Supreme Creator, realized that it would be impossible to experience anything as long as he remained in his original state as "all that is", one without a second. When you are everything, there are no others to have experiences with! It would be like playing a game of chess with yourself, turning the board around after every move because you are controlling both the white and the black pieces.

There was only one solution. God would need to forget his own divine identity as the supreme whole and descend into a voluntary state of amnesia, believing himself to be partial and limited creatures, objects, and experiences. While doing so made him forget his divinity, it enabled him to finally satisfy his loving and creative impulse toward expression, expansion, and experience. The first chapter of the Aitareya Upanishad describes this beautifully: "In the beginning all this was Atman (the supreme formless lord or pure consciousness), one and without a second…he willed himself to create the worlds". The Chandogya Upanishad further describes that this formless and changeless supreme divinity decided "I shall be many. I shall be born".

In a single instant, before the parameters of time and space existed, God created the greatest, vastest, and most glorious game of all time by asking himself just one question: "Who Am I?"

The Book of Exodus captures God's elegant and succinct answer to the question: "I AM THAT I AM".

God's answer was not "I am something". It was simply "I AM". In other words, in an instant, God defined himself as "I AM X", where X includes everything and every possible experience. God himself is I AM, the totality. All seemingly separate objects and creatures in existence are partial expressions of God limiting himself in order to gain unique experiences. Being a human offers a different experience compared to being an animal. Being an alien lifeform on a planet outside earth offers a different experience compared to being a human. Being a male offers a different experience compared to being a female. The possibilities are infinite, endless, and already "coded" into the very fabric of creation. There is nothing left to make, and as the old saying goes, there is nothing new under the sun, including the sun itself! I AM is greater than any person, place, object, or experience because all things depend on I AM, but I AM depends on none of them. I AM, or pure consciousness, is the only independent reality. As Jesus put it, "Before Abraham was, I AM!". In other words, men, objects, planets, universes, and even the time-space fabric of reality are merely dependent objects inside the fundamental reality of pure consciousness or formless existence.

When God answered the question "Who Am I?", all of creation popped into existence. The dimensions of time and space came into being as a canvas for experience. And every possible experience God could have, meaning every possible reality, timeline, universe, and sequence of events, instantly materialized into physical reality. Humans, animals, natural landscapes, planets, universes, and galaxies all appeared instantly. Moreover, all possible variants of these entities, across all timeliness, and every combination and permutation of events, were created in a flash.

In other words, by declaring himself as I AM, God created an infinite playground by forgetting his own true identity as ALL THAT IS and descending into an infinite number of points of consciousness, each equipped to enjoy an infinite number of experiences. Every plant, insect, bird, animal, and human represents a divine expression of God experiencing himself through that particular channel.

Now, here is the most remarkable part of this story of divine creation. God had to forget himself to become man, so you are a ray of God as well! **You are the almighty creator, vested and imbued with his infinite power and wisdom**. Every piece of God contains the whole of God, a principle that is reflected in physical creation (for instance, each cell in the body contains the DNA template for the entire body, not just that particular cell). You have simply forgotten who you are because you chose to. You chose to forget who you were in order to have the experience of being human. If you remembered the fact that you are actually God or ALL THAT IS, you would never be able to properly enjoy and experience what it feels like to be a separate creature. The experience of being human would feel like a hazy video game or simulation, rather than a rich and realistic experience that feels "solid". Your amnesia of your Godhood was necessary and something YOU VOLUNTARILY CHOSE in order to gain rich experiences of reality. God had to forget himself to truly become man, hoping that man would eventually realize himself to be God.

Many have wondered what the purpose of the universe is. You might even wonder how that question is relevant to obtaining your desires. You might be tempted to think you don't want spiritual truths and simply want to know how to earn more money, get the girl or guy of your dreams, or become famous. However, as you will see, understanding the full picture of Paramorphing makes it infinitely easier to materialize any object or experience you may desire. And you will also see that the greatest desire among them all is to recognize who you truly are.

The beauty is that the universe is inherently meaningless and purposeless. It is simply God playing. This affords you the wonderful freedom and right as a son or daughter of God: THE UNIVERSE HAS WHATEVER MEANING YOU GIVE IT, AND NOTHING MORE. This means that you have full creative license to choose your life to be EXACTLY what you desire.

Desires are not evil or contradictory to spiritual progress, as many traditions mistakenly teach. Rather, it is an incomplete picture of the full truth. ALL DESIRES stem from the one and ONLY fundamental desire in all of creation: FOR GOD, THE CREATOR, TO KNOW HIMSELF. All desires, urges, and impulses are divine because the creator wishes to know all that he is, piece by piece, eventually realizing that he is the whole, all that is. Ultimately, it is never the desire itself that is satisfying, but the fulfillment of it that produces peace, joy, happiness, and satisfaction.

Given that no desire is objectively wrong, one may then wonder whether morality matters at all. Moral rules and codes of conduct were established for the benefit of those who have forgotten their true nature as children of God. Once you know yourself to be God, Source, the creative fountain of love that is infinite and unlimited, you will realize that you do not need to lie, cheat, steal, harm, manipulate, or coerce others to gain anything you want. If you would like to enjoy opulence while adding value to the lives of others, Paramorphing will provide you with great wealth generated through a profoundly successful business. If you wish to enjoy the physical pleasures of a romantic relationship, Paramorphing will effortlessly bring an ideal partner into your life who harmonizes with you in every possible way.

With this in mind, it is tempting to wonder if one can simply become desireless, and stay in the desireless state of pure consciousness, I AM, without wanting anything. The ancient traditions that speak of self-realization and non-duality are not wrong. Advaita Vedanta, for instance, speaks of self-realization, or spiritual enlightenment, the point at which man overcomes his delusion of being a separate and limited creature and realizes he is actually one with the entire cosmos, recognizing that everything he perceives is merely a broadcast of his own mind.

There is nothing wrong with staying in the pure state of I AM, enjoying the indescribable peace, bliss, and pure love that flows from this state of Godhood. However, it is not necessary. As we will discuss through this book, you are ALREADY God. Desires are the divine urge of the Creator, seeking to experientially enjoy himself through you! As we will discuss shortly, there are infinite parallel lives that you are living HERE and NOW, and desires, especially compelling or strong desires, are simply very close parallel realities that are "bleeding" into your present reality. Rejoice! If you have a truly burning desire, it is quite literally MEANT FOR YOU, belongs to you, and there is ALREADY a version of you in a parallel reality, as solid and tangible as the world you see right now, experiencing the desire. You can very well know that you are already God, yet still enjoy the world of form by embracing your desires, knowing that they are already yours. In fact, by remaining light, detached, and playful rather than desperately craving for or obsessing over your desires, you will find that they ironically appear rapidly in your physical reality, without friction or struggle.

You are inherently worthy of any and all desires because the infinite kingdom of God, which contains all possibilities, timelines, and experiences has been given to you as a GIFT. As Jesus put it succinctly, "Fear not, little flock; for it is your Father's good pleasure to give you the kingdom". You do not have to strive, struggle, manifest, attempt, or "prove" your worthiness. Now, of course, if you believe that you must strive and struggle, you will simply create a reality in which you strive and struggle. Paramorphing is the language of God, and God's language is a divine translating printer that simply transforms your imaginative self-concept (who you truly feel that you are) into physical reality. Because God is utterly simple and perfectly honest, your reality will reflect not what you say or claim to be, but what you GENUINELY FEEL yourself to be. The divine printer has no motives of its own and operates with crystal clarity. Verbally saying you are healthy while internally feeling frustration toward your body will not enable you to experience health, for example. What you truly internally feel yourself to be is exactly what the world will show you.

Most people who have had spiritual awakenings, even preliminary ones, clearly sense, intuit, and glimpse that they are much more than their physical body or mind. Some develop clairvoyance and other "supernatural" abilities. Some get glimpses or visions of what they believe to be future events or past lives. Others still go through near-death experiences (NDEs) or out-of-body experiences (OBEs), in which they find themselves experiencing other realms and realities.

However, there is no future or past, though the limited human mind can only think in these terms. In reality, there is only the eternal I AM of God, which is HERE and NOW. This means that every lifeline, timeline, sequence of experiences, and universe in which you could find yourself was not only created in a flash when God declared himself to be I AM but also exists HERE and NOW, as solid and tangible as the physical world you see before you!

Just think, for a moment, about what that means. Your past lives are all happening NOW. Heaven and hell are happening NOW. The construction of the pyramids in 3000 BC is actually happening NOW. You have had lifetimes as servants and kings, men and women, warriors, and artists, and they are all happening NOW. There is no future either; the year 4000 is also happening NOW. Your lives as non-human creatures in other alien realms, solar systems, and galaxies, including realms that have more than 3 dimensions as we have on Earth, are also happening NOW.

In other words, there is no future or past. The Supreme Creator, with one wave of his cosmic palm, brought everything into creation. All of it exists HERE and NOW inside the Eternal Cosmic Library. Everything that is, was, or will be, has already been produced.

This is crucial to understand because it goes against everything that most people believe about their existence. God has no time or space. God exists beyond time, or NOW, and beyond space, or HERE. God is HERE and NOW, but even these terms are likely to be misconstrued by the human mind which can only categorize objects, things, and experiences into a time-space 3-dimensional framework. God being HERE and NOW can more simply be conveyed as "God Is". God is existence itself, total, infinitely comprehensive, and containing all things.

At first glance, this seems ludicrous and quite literally impossible to believe. And for good reason: The human mind is not supposed to be able to grasp eternity. It was designed to focus on

ONE particular lifetime in ONE particular timeline on ONE particular realm with its rules and parameters (in this case, living on planet Earth). Each lifetime you experience is merely a single reality permutation of experiences that you observe and consider to be "your life".

However, all the other experiences, lifetimes, and realities you have encountered or could encounter in the "future" or "past" are also happening NOW. **We call these infinite unobserved realities Parallel Reality Layers (PRLs).** They all exist eternally in God's Eternal Cosmic Library.

The most magical and wondrous fact is that YOU CAN ACCESS ANY PRL NOW. This is the foundation of Paramorphing, which is the science of morphing, or switching, from one PRL to another. You are God temporarily enjoying a specific human experience, which you take to be your "real life", but you still have access to the Eternal Cosmic Library where all things, experiences, and possibilities exist forever. Nothing can be destroyed, though it might appear that way in the world of forms. The divine template for all things exists externally, immune to damage or destruction. As the Book of Isaiah succinctly puts it, "they shall not hurt or destroy in all my holy mountain".

So, what does all this mean in practical terms?

Yes indeed, it means that there is ALREADY a version of you that is wealthy. One that is healthy. Still, another version is a champion athlete. There are also versions of you that are tired, miserable, unhealthy, and absolutely destitute. Each of these PRLs exists for you to choose from. Remember, PRLs are eternal because all possibilities exist forever in God's Eternal Cosmic Library. You cannot destroy or oppose any of them because to destroy anything would be to destroy God, which is impossible since God is everlasting existence. However, you can most certainly choose the PRL that you desire to experience! This is your divine right as a child of God to whom all things are given.

If I were to ask a person who she is, she might say something like: "I am Kelly Miller. I work in real estate as a broker. It pays the bills although I wish I earn a bit more. My folks are of Irish and Scottish descent and my family has been in the United States for the last 3 years, since 2012. I miss being in Europe and wish I were back there. My husband John and I want children but have had issues conceiving. My hobbies include tennis, playing the guitar, and surfing yet I've had some trouble of late due to my arthritis and asthma that have slowed me down a bit".

However, what Kelly might not realize is that this is merely ONE reality permutation that she happens to be experiencing now. It is not absolute or the only reality. There are other PRLs happening right here and right now, just as solid and tangible as the life she described above.

While all of Kelly's lives are happening now (and it is possible for her to access any of them), she most likely does not care about visiting the past or traveling to the future. If you asked her what she truly wanted, she would probably say more money, better health, and freedom.

The good news is that everything Kelly wants has already been created and is available for her to choose from, like dishes at an infinite cosmic buffet. There is a PRL where she works the same job as a real estate broker but makes a salary that is 50% higher. There is another PRL where she makes 4x her current income by running her own real estate brokerage. There is yet another PRL where she has an award-winning television show about real estate fixer-uppers and enjoys global stardom and fame. Regarding health, there is an already existing PRL in which Kelly has no asthma or arthritis. Now, of course, there are also "worse" PRLs in which Kelly has much poorer health than she experiences in her present reality, or has no job at all. In reality, in God's eyes of infinity, no

PRL is "better" or "worse", but from Kelly's standpoint, it would be preferable to be healthy and wealthy rather than sick and poor.

So how do you move from one PRL to another? This is the holy grail of creation. We will now push back the curtains and reveal the ancient secrets to harnessing your inner divinity to move from one reality to another. In truth, though, you are not "moving" anywhere because everything exists here and now, including all the infinite PRLs you could choose from.

Therefore, we use the term Paramorphing, which simply means morphing from one Parallel Reality Layer to another. You aren't going anywhere, as you are the very center of reality, and all possibilities exist within you here and now. Rather, by molding your inner conception of who you declare yourself to be, who you say you are, you "glide", or morph, from one PRL to another. Let us now begin.

* * * * * * * * * *

Chapter 3: The Core Paramorphing Process

To Paramorph from one Parallel Reality Layer (PRL) to another, all you have to do is declare and feel that you are in your desired PRL, with certainty and absolute conviction that you are in the new reality HERE and NOW and that you already have whatever it is that you desired.

Congratulations. That's it. If you can do this perfectly already, there's no need to read the rest of the book. If you can say "I am a Fortune 500 CEO" and instantly find yourself to be a Fortune 500 CEO, or if you can say "I am married to Person Z" and instantly find yourself married to Person Z, you are a wizard or a saint, someone who naturally and intuitively understands how to shift from one PRL to another. Is this possible? Most certainly. But for nearly all humans other than advanced mystics, their reality doesn't appear to change quite so easily or instantly. All things are possible with God, and that quite literally means ALL THINGS. A person can decree "I am a millionaire" with absolute conviction and find their bank balance updated instantly to show a million dollars. However, what prevents most people from doing this and finding such a result?

There is ONE divine God-mind or absolute reality that eternally exists. You can call this absolute reality "Source", for it is the basis of all things. This reality is pure consciousness, or I AM, as we discussed previously. This divine God-mind is linked to the Eternal Cosmic Library, where "templates" for every possible object, person, creature, experience, and universe already exist. In other words, every PRL has an indestructible, eternally existing template that can always be accessed, whether or not that PRL has been called into physical reality.

The entire world that you experience as "reality", including your own body, the people around you, your possessions, and even your environment, are merely STALE printouts of one particular template from the Eternal Cosmic Library. Even if the entire life you consider to be yours was destroyed, or even if the planet as a whole was destroyed, it could be brought back into physical experience in a flash because only printouts can be destroyed. Physical reality is a printout. The PRL templates in the Eternal Cosmic Library CANNOT be destroyed. So yes, even if Earth were to suddenly be blown up, or humankind was wiped out by a massive asteroid, Earth and all the humans on it could be recreated instantly because the template for planet Earth and the template for any and all possible humans exists in God's Eternal Cosmic Library. As an analogy, suppose you have printed out a particular document, and you happen to accidentally shred it. Would you fret? Of course not. As long as you have the digital file on your computer, you can quickly make a new copy. God's Eternal Cosmic Library contains "digital templates" of all possible realities, and unlike digital files on Earth, no divine template can ever be destroyed.

The next logical question, obviously, is how do you pick a PRL template from the Eternal Cosmic Library and translate it into physical reality? You are not merely interested in knowing that there is an already-existing parallel reality in which you are healthy, rich, married to your dream partner, and so forth. You want to experience it in the flesh.

You are currently playing a particular PRL template from the Eternal Cosmic Library which has "hardened" into the physical reality you see in your daily life and take to be "the real world". In truth, there is no objective reality. What you are seeing is merely your mind displaying your chosen PRL. In other words, everything you perceive is an illusion constructed by your mind.

Take a few minutes to dwell on this deeply before proceeding further, because it is foundational to Paramorphing. THERE IS NO OBJECTIVE WORLD OUTSIDE OF YOU. There isn't a world "out there". You aren't a small human living in a larger city or community on a planet called Earth in the Solar System in the Milky Way galaxy. Your body, Earth, and even the Milky Way are projections of your own mind and THEY ARE ALL WITHIN YOU.

The poet Rumi said it beautifully: "You are not a drop in the ocean but the ocean in a drop"You are pure I AM, infinite possibilities, that merely HAPPENS to be experiencing one particular PRL template now that you identified with so strongly that it crystallized into what you consider to be the "real world". However, it isn't permanently real. It can be changed. This is a beautiful thing, for it allows you to discover who you truly are: The creator!

At first, the human mind scoffs at this and finds it to be comical at best and ludicrously delusional at worst, but it is reality. Whatever you see, witness, and experience is a projection of YOUR OWN MIND. Your own mind is playing a particular PRL template. Therefore, if you want to change anything about your life, whether it's your financial situation, health, relationship with other people, or anything else, there is only one person to change: YOU! More specifically, you need to stop selecting the current PRL that contains an "undesirable" reality and simply choose the already-existing PRL that contains your heart's desires.

Each day, when you go into deep sleep, the world that you consider to be real disappears. In deep sleep, you have no sense of being a person. You have no sense of your body. You have no sense of other people, and you most certainly do not perceive your city or the fact that you're on a planet called Earth. In deep sleep, you are pure consciousness, I AM, or God! Yes, in deep sleep, you unite with the Eternal Cosmic Library or divine mind of God in which all PRLs exist eternally. It is ONLY when you awaken that you, in an instant, become aware of your identity as a person, with a name, a family, a certain set of possessions, a particular set of life views and beliefs, on a certain planet, and so forth. You spend the day believing yourself to be a human being in a particular set of life circumstances, and when you go to sleep, the entire world that you took to be so solid disappears until you reawaken.

A PRL template is simply a collection of beliefs and the corresponding world or experience of physical reality that is created as a result. It is how you define yourself and the world around you. For instance, your current PRL may be "I am a human man named Eric Smith living in the United States. With hard work and luck, I feel a person can succeed in life. Money certainly doesn't grow on trees". Of course, this is just a small snippet of a person's currently experienced PRL. In reality, every person has countless beliefs, some visible, and some unknown even to them unless they truly examine themselves. For example, a person may on the surface say that they believe they wish to earn more money, but deep down have a latent underlying belief that money is the root of all evil and that desiring wealth is immoral or evil in some way. You have beliefs about your own personality, people as a whole, specific groups of people, particular individuals, money, health, life purpose, and nearly every other thing imaginable. And it is these beliefs that constitute the PRL template that gets displayed as your life experience of physical reality, each and every day! There is no "real world" out there. You are projecting ALL OF IT, right here and right now, from your own mind and the PRL template that you are playing.

Observe yourself carefully right before you go to sleep, and right before you awaken. As you go to sleep, if you simply maintain a relaxed but attentive state, you will feel your mind start "descending" toward your heart. It cannot be fully expressed in words but can easily be observed. As you fall asleep, the mind goes and rests in the heart, which is the seat of the Eternal Cosmic Library where ALL PRL templates exist. As you awaken in the morning, if you maintain the same relaxed but attentive state, you will feel your mind "rising" from the heart toward the head. The head is the opposite of the heart. The brain's job is to display ONE PRL template, which then becomes the "real world" that you perceive with your 5 senses.

Why does reality appear mostly the same when you wake up each morning? It is because your head is displaying almost the same PRL template each day because your core beliefs are unchanged. You have certain fundamental core beliefs that are nearly unshakeable. For example, you have a deep assumption and conviction that you live on a planet called Earth in a particular country. You have a deep belief that you belong to a particular race and gender. You have a deep belief that you have certain close relatives and family members with certain characteristics. You also believe that you are a human being and that objects on your realm, planet Earth, follow certain predictable patterns according to certain natural laws; birds can fly while humans can't, and an object thrown up in the ground comes back down due to gravity. To you, such core beliefs are so "obvious" and "unshakeable" that they appear to feel like solid reality. These core beliefs are why you wake up each day to a reality that feels predictable, in the same family, on the same planet, with the same natural laws.

The head and heart are perfect complementary opposites. The head has the ability to PICK any particular PRL template but does not have the energetic fuel to convert it from a template into physical reality. The heart has the energetic fuel to convert ANY PRL template into physical reality, but it has no preferences and choices around what PRL should be picked.

We use the terms "heart" and "head" here, but we are not referring to the pure physical organs. We are referring to the nature of the energetic field contained in both these energetic centers, which flows through the respective organs. The energy field of the brain, located in the head, is the energy of selection and choice, while the energy field of the heart, located in the chest, is the energy of materialization, capable of powering any chosen PRL into physical experience.

Here is the core Paramorphing process, in a nutshell.

In order to Paramorph from one PRL to another, you must pick a newly desired PRL, and absolutely feel that PRL is already here, walking in the consciousness of already being what you formerly desired, no matter what your eyes show you. You must fully and truly feel that you are already in your new PRL no matter what your senses show you. For instance, suppose you suffer from chronic dermatitis in your current PRL, and you wish to move into the PRL in which you are perfectly healthy. The first step is to be conscious of being a healthy person and embody this role fully. Paramorphing does not reward merely thinking of a desired PRL, imitating a desired PRL halfheartedly, or waffling back and forth between the current PRL and the desired PRL. God is absolute honesty and sincerity, and when he becomes something in the world of form, he becomes it FULLY. In other words, if you desire health, but merely pay lip service to the PRL of being healthy while deep down believing you are still unhealthy, you cannot Paramorph into your desired PRL. You may fool billions of men and women, but you can never fool God, who is infinite intelligence. Thus, you must mentally and emotionally embody the new PRL. If the new PRL is "I AM healthy and have beautifully clear skin", how would you naturally feel? You would feel happy when seeing your arms. Internally, you would feel happy, grateful, and perhaps relieved to see your beautiful skin. You would walk around without any self-consciousness about your arms or how others might see them. In other words, you are not thinking ABOUT the new PRL as something to attain in "the future"; you are thinking AFTER the new PRL by assertively claiming it and appropriating it as your new identity NOW.

Remember that time does not exist in truth; there is only the ETERNAL PRESENT. In this NOW moment, you can be in EITHER the old PRL OR the new PRL. You cannot be in two PRLs at once. You are either healthy now, or unhealthy now. If you are waiting for a future in which you become healthy, that future will never come, because when it comes, it will be NOW.

Does it feel "delusional" to believe and embody a PRL that you can't physically see with your senses yet? That's ok. Don't worry about it. Your only conscious job is to faithfully appropriate the new PRL mentally and emotionally, in your imagination. All you have to do is BE CONSCIOUS OF NOW HAVING whatever you desire. Your imagined state of consciousness as "I AM HEALTHY" and the thoughts and emotions that follow it, are the TRUE reality because the physical world that you observe is just a DEAD printout of PRL templates that exist in the Eternal Cosmic Library of God. Remember, all PRLs already exist! Therefore, if you can imagine a PRL, for instance, a world in which your skin is clear and you are healthy, that reality exists and is every bit as solid and tangible as your current PRL. You simply aren't seeing and perceiving it yet since it has been veiled from your senses due to your current PRL and its dominant belief, which is "I AM SUFFERING FROM DERMATITIS".

What if you wish to feel healthy, and adopt the consciousness of "I AM SOMEONE WHO WANTS TO GET HEALTHY"? Remember, God never judges what you select. The divine power of Paramorphing is a perfect input-in and input-out printer that takes precisely the PRL template you feed it and spits it out into physical reality. If your state of consciousness is "I WANT TO BE HEALTHY", you will morph yourself into a physical reality in which you…merely want to be healthy, but are NOT necessarily healthy! This is why it is CRITICAL to adopt the consciousness of ALREADY being in the PRL you desire, instead of being someone who wants, desires, craves, or is "working toward" the new PRL.

Wanting, desiring, craving, trying, working toward, and thinking about something are synonyms for NOT HAVING IT. If your PRL template is "NOT HAVING IT", the perfect printer of God's divine mind, which faithfully spits out ONLY the precise inputs you feed it, will create a physical reality in which you DO NOT HAVE whatever you desire.

Humans on earth, from the time they are young, are taught to dismiss imagination as "make-believe" due to the ignorance of the adults around them. In reality, imagination is the FOUNDATIONAL CAUSE of all reality. Everything you see around you is imagination, a PRL template of beliefs that you persisted in long enough to materialize as the physical world you now perceive. All PRL templates exist, but only the ones you persistently believe in actualize as physical reality.

The head's job ends there. From this point on, the work of materializing the new PRL into physical existence is the job of the heart, which has access to God's Eternal Cosmic Library of infinite possibilities and thus, knows how to bring any PRL into existence in the most efficient way possible. The heart, it is important to note, is connected to ALL REALITIES and ALL POSSIBILITIES but has no preferences, so it can only reflect the PRL you choose and embody.

Remember, God is not only infinite love but also limitless intelligence; a thousand of the smartest human minds put together would not be able to achieve a thousandth of a percent of the power, potency, and capability of God's infinite wisdom, which can quite literally morph time, space, and physical reality itself to seemingly magically bring about any PRL into physical reality. Trying to coerce or force the sequence of events toward a new PRL using the limited human mind often causes frustration, delays, and irritation.

The limited human mind can, at best, conceive of a few ways toward realizing a PRL and breathing it into physical existence. The divine mind of God quite literally has an infinite number of routes to do so and also knows the most efficient route involving parameters that the limited human mind cannot know of even if it wanted to. If one clings to maintaining control over the process, the mind impedes the process of morphing into a new reality, and the heart, connected to God's infinite intelligence, cannot breathe and execute its task, causing delays in seeing the new PRL one has chosen.

The "real world" that appears when you are awake is merely one PRL template that your mind has selected from the infinite PRLs in God's Eternal Cosmic Library and is now projecting as your "real world" experience.

In reality, however, none of your beliefs are objectively real or permanent. Only I AM, pure consciousness or existence, is objectively real; all other beliefs can be changed and only exist subjectively based on you, the observer! There are PRLs in which you live on a different planet. In a different year. With a different family. There are PRLs in which you can touch fire and not be harmed, walk on water, and defy gravity. This is not mere speculation or wishful thinking. There are individuals right now, even on Earth, who are capable of such "superhuman" feats. The ancient Vedic seers and clairvoyants called these abilities, such as being able to see something thousands of miles away or change one's physical size, "siddhis". There are people who can fly and those who can walk on water. You, however, do not see these parallel realities due to your existing belief structure which you maintain day after day, assuming it to be absolute truth when it is merely ONE possibility out of an infinite pool of possibilities that all exist in you. If you do not believe such abilities are possible, that belief structure will FILTER OUT any reality in which you can observe such feats!

The takeaway is that you are never "seeing" an objective world. You are merely seeing a world composed of your existing core belief structure, which forms your currently experienced PRL.

However, you do know that it is possible to morph PRLs because you have done so. You may have considered someone you knew to be distant and cranky, even a potential foe, for a long time, but a sudden moment of bonding at a party might have made this person your friend. Now, going forward, you would see a world in which your core beliefs (like being a human on earth) are unchanged, but one small belief (your perception of one person who is now your friend rather than an enemy) has changed. In other words, you have morphed into a new PRL that is very close to your old PRL.

Now, why is this possible? Because the IDEA that a person could change from an enemy to a friend is BELIEVABLE to you. You believe that this is possible, and so you can switch to a new PRL where you now believe a certain person is a friend rather than an enemy. To your human mind, which assumes that your life is simply one "track", you will perceive the change in a linear fashion, believing that particular person was an enemy "in the past" but now "is your friend". In reality, BOTH those tracks exist perpetually. The PRL in which that person is your enemy exists perpetually in God's Eternal Cosmic Library, as does the PRL in which that person is your friend.

You are not changing the person and they have not changed from being an enemy to being a friend. Rather, you USED to observe the PRL in which they were an enemy, and now you observe the PRL in which they are a friend. But just because you are observing one PRL doesn't mean the others cease to exist! All realities exist perpetually. Even when you believe the person is now your friend, the PRL in which they are your enemy exists in a reality just as solid and tangible as the world you perceive now. However, your new belief structure of this person being a friend causes that other reality to disappear from your world experience.

Now, assuming you have selected your newly chosen PRL, how does your world actually transform from your existing PRL to the new one? This is something your human mind cannot know and is not meant to know. The head's job is not to direct sequences of events in time and space. The head's job is merely to choose the new PRL and rest at ease knowing it is done. It is your heart's job to connect to the divine mind of God, the Eternal Cosmic Library, and employ the infinite intelligence of the creator to shift your physical circumstances to your newly chosen PRL in the most efficient and natural way possible.

As such, the only real question anyone should ask is WHICH PRL ARE YOU PLACING YOUR ATTENTION ON here and now? The answer to this question determines your entire life experience. You are EVERYTHING, literally, EVERYTHING, yet your attention and self-conception, who you define yourself as, determines the tiny slice of God's eternity that you experience in your current lifetime.

Based on the examples above, it is clear that is easier for most people to believe some realities over others. Most people can believe that they can switch to a PRL where they see a 10% salary bump within a year. However, they have less belief that they can switch to a PRL where their salary doubles by the end of the year. And with regards to a financial windfall such as winning the national lottery or becoming a billionaire, most people have almost no belief that it can be done. Similarly, in the domain of health, most people would find it believable to switch to a PRL in which they lose 5 pounds by the end of the year, while they would find it utterly unbelievable to switch to a PRL in which they win Mr. Olympia.

However, there is one extremely important thing to note. From the standpoint of God, the divine mind with access to the Eternal Cosmic Library, all PRL templates are EQUALLY EASY TO ACCESS. From the standpoint of God, there is no difference in the "difficulty" or "impressiveness" of winning a $50 or $50,000,000 lottery. From the standpoint of God's mind, in which all PRL templates have ALREADY been created and exist eternally, the PRL template in which a person has Stage 4 cancer is as easy to access as the PRL template in which that same person is perfectly healthy.

It is only to the limited human mind that certain PRLs seem "believable" and "achievable" while others seem "unbelievable" or "impossible". To God, no PRL is "better" or "worse". Remember, God is simply I AM. God is beyond notions of good and evil and transcends measurements and judgments.

As the poet Rumi put it so beautifully, "beyond good and evil, there is a field. I will meet you there".

This field is the divine mind of God, connected to the Eternal Cosmic Library in which all PRLs exist and in which all things are possible.

From the human standpoint, it appears that certain PRLs are more achievable or believable than others. It is entirely possible for a person to have stronger beliefs and convictions about themselves in certain life domains while having weaker convictions in other areas. For example, a person might believe themselves to be capable of acquiring great wealth but may lack that same conviction when it comes to romantic relationships. Others may feel great prowess in their romantic relationships and believe they can effortlessly attract great partners while they lack the same conviction in curing health issues, for instance.

The Eternal Cosmic Library, the divine mind of God, has all possibilities, so all possible PRLs exist in your personal PRL library as well, as you are a ray of God made in God's image. You are equidistant to ALL PRLs but your human beliefs cause certain PRLs to appear easier or more realistic to achieve than others.

That is the beauty of Paramorphing, the language of God. God is beyond time, space, and linear change. God's name is I AM, and I AM can become ANYTHING. When you access the holy center of your being, I AM, and decide you are a new identity, you quite literally bend and warp time and space INSTANTLY, here and now. Wormholes aren't science fiction. They truly do exist, and the way you create magical miracles that defy the 3D laws of time and space is by going to the center of God within you. As Jesus asked his disciples, "Who do you say I AM?". In other words, who do you declare yourself to be? For example, when a formerly nervous woman with a history and identity of attracting abusive relationships discards that state of victimhood and boldly decides that I AM A WORTHY WOMAN WHO ATTRACTS AMAZING MEN INTO MY LIFE, and sticks to this new identity no matter what, time and space will literally bend, warp, and collapse to make her new PRL a physical reality.

In Paramorphing, there are only two fundamental energetic forces that determine how humans create reality: Faith and Friction. That's it. These two primary forces determine how any life experience is created, and all success or failure in obtaining your heart's desires depends on only these two factors. At any given time, you are embodying the energetic state of a particular PRL. Suppose you wish to move to a new PRL and you start mentally and imaginatively embodying it at this moment. At any moment, you are either resting in the old PRL or the new PRL; you cannot straddle, because if you are honest, you will notice you are either living in the consciousness of having the thing/object/experience you desired (the new PRL) or not having it (the old PRL). When the ratio of your faith to friction reaches or exceeds 51 : 49, your new PRL will become a physical reality. This is an absolute law. The wonderful news is that "perfect" and "doubtless" faith is not necessary. It is natural to have doubts; when they arise, simply gently put your attention and awareness back on the new PRL you wish to now embody. **When your belief in your new PRL becomes your default energetic state (51% or more of your imaginative self-concept), you Paramorph to your new PRL.**

Faith is the intangible LOVING CONVICTION of claiming a new PRL and deciding it is your reality. Faith represents absolute belief and certainty that a new PRL is yours. From your current PRL, any other PRL is EQUALLY EASY to claim, because claiming a new PRL is your God-given right. Remember, from the perspective of the divine mind, God's Eternal Cosmic Library, no PRL is "superior" or "inferior". They are all equal. In God's eyes, the lifeline of being a fit and handsome billionaire is inherently no worthier than that of a poor man who is riddled with diseases. So, CLAIMING is the part of you that identifies with your inner divinity, which is tied to all possible PRLs and experiences.

The catch, however, is energetic friction. In the pure God state, you can claim anything and instantly jump into that PRL because you are all that is. You are equidistant to all possibilities. However, when you came down from your true Godhood into human form, you forgot about your true glory. You were born into a human body, and as you grew up on Earth, your environment molded your belief system. Perhaps you were raised in an abusive household that made you feel unworthy and created the belief that love was something you had to work hard for. Perhaps you grew up in a household where family members always complained about money or health, instilling beliefs in you that perfect health and abundant wealth are inaccessible to you. On top of all this, Earth is a realm where matter is slow to change and appears "dense" and "objectively real" due to the parameter of linear time, which can discourage a person or make it appear like they are making no progress toward their newly chosen PRL. Doubt, in short, is the foundation of friction. All these factors create energetic friction, which slows down or prevents you from morphing into your newly chosen reality.

Faith is the force of PURE LOVE. Friction is the force of PURE FEAR. The heart is the seat of your God-mind, where there is only faith because all possibilities exist in the Eternal Cosmic Library. The head is the seat of your limited human-mind, which is besieged and plagued by fear, doubts, limitation, worries, and lack of belief and conviction.

In other words, the secret and essence of Paramorphing consists of claiming your desired PRL while eliminating the

energetic friction that impedes you from morphing into your new state. The next chapter will explain the different flavors of energetic friction and how to overcome them. But before that, you may wonder: Why do we choose human lives? If we, as sons and daughters of God, can pick any reality, why would we choose a realm like Earth in which there is so much energetic friction that seemingly delays us from achieving the things we want?

Of all the realms it is possible to experience, Earth is one of the densest realms to live a life on. It is akin to playing the game of life in "advanced" or "expert" mode. While I cannot prove this to you with objective evidence, I can offer you the spiritual truths I was allowed to glimpse and also encourage you to read testimonies of people who have visited other realms, astral planets, and even what people call heaven following near-death experiences. On other realms and planets, life is substantially more harmonious, peaceful, and abundant, and these realms are less dense, meaning you can simply claim a PRL and morph into it immediately.

For example, in a heavenly realm, it is easy to understand and believe that all things are possible because even a person with comparatively little faith or belief can decree "I own a mansion" and it will pop up right before them. On a heavenly realm, one may simply wish for an astral tree to produce a certain type of fruit, or for the climate to change from cold to warm, and all this can happen instantly. It is beyond the scope of this book to discuss astral realms, but let it suffice to say that they exist. In such realms, it is clearly and palpably visible that the so-called material world is not solid at all, but merely a function of imagination. The inhabitants of those realms know that by simply changing their imagination and claiming new PRLs, their external reality will shift quickly and predictably. Not much faith is required; even those with little conviction can easily change their reality because these realms are easily malleable via thought.

On Earth, the very same force of faith applies, but the high density and steep level of energetic friction on this planet mean that you will have to persist far stronger and with much more conviction to shift to your desired PRL, especially if it is a PRL that you find it hard to believe you can have or move to.

As a child of God, you wanted a challenge; while "younger" souls choose less dense and far more harmonious realms and universes to start their spiritual journey, you wanted to experience your divinity in the deepest and richest way, so you agreed to undertake the greatest challenge by coming to Earth, a realm which requires you to undergo so much temporary amnesia that you feel like you are a small, separate creature facing a vast and unpredictable outside world. I know this because the realm I am originally from, where I had my "last" birth before incarnating on Earth, is one such astral paradise. On these other realms, there is not much amnesia; the souls there do limit themselves to a degree because God necessarily has to limit himself in some way to experience reality, but they truly and deeply know that they are connected to the Eternal Cosmic Library, the mind of God, and that all PRLs are possible to claim. They knew that underneath all superficial appearances, there is only the one divine mind of God, from which all changes and experiences are possible. Earth, however, involves so much forgetfulness that a soul born on Earth almost completely forgets that it is God. Most earth souls are totally unaware that they have access to the infinite Eternal Cosmic Library which contains all PRLs. Only a soul that wanted a true challenge would choose to come to Earth, which is a realm for those who wish to test their faith under the densest and most trying circumstances.

However, there is a benefit to all this. By playing the game of life on expert mode, you develop a level of precision and mastery in creating reality that you simply would not develop in gentler realms. For example, take the analogy of cameras. If you use a smartphone camera, it will easily take decent photos because it automatically adjusts factors such as lighting, shutter speed, auto-focus, and others. Even a photography novice can take an attractive photo quickly on a smartphone, but he will lack a true understanding of why he took a good-quality photo. On the other hand, if you were to use a professional-grade film camera, you would have to adjust all these factors yourself. Nothing would be done for you, so to speak, and a novice attempting to take images would struggle immensely at first. However, as he manually masters parameters such as lighting, lens options, and focus, which were previously done automatically for him on the smartphone, he gains a truly masterful understanding of what creates a great photograph. Earth is the film camera, a realm that tests your faith and conviction in the deepest and most challenging way, allowing you to learn the most about creating reality. **It is the equivalent of a PhD thesis in learning how to master physical reality.**

Does that mean Earth has limitations on what can be created compared to other realms? Are we "constrained" in the range of PRLs we can shift to? The answer is absolutely not. On lighter realms, as we have discussed, a person can quickly think of an object, such as a flute, and have it instantly materialize in the palm of her hand. **The same is true here; it is possible, even on Earth, to instantly materialize an item by merely thinking that you have it in your palm.** From the standpoint of your divine God-mind, there is nothing hard about doing this because you are simply shifting from the current PRL in which you don't have the object, to the new PRL in which you have the object. Both PRLs already exist in the Eternal Cosmic Library, the divine mind of God.

However, from the standpoint of your human mind, it is an impressive feat to override the friction caused by doubts that such reality-bending feats can actually be done. Saints, mystics, wizards, and others who have mastered control over their minds can, however, perform such feats. They can materialize objects out of thin air, appear in multiple places at once as demonstrated by Sai Baba of Shirdi, raise the dead back to life as shown by Mahavatar Babaji, walk on water like Jesus, drink poison without dying like Shiva, and lift mountains with their pinkies, as Krishna did with

Mount Govardhan. They can also order objects to move around in time and space, as ancient architects did to build superhuman structures without modern technology such as cranes and hydraulic forklifts. To God, all things are possible. If you can imagine a particular scene, there is a PRL in which your imagination already exists as a solid reality. There are no exceptions.

While Earth is a comparatively dense realm, this doesn't limit you in any way if you maintain faith and conviction in your desired PRL by embodying it NOW. Remember, I AM is the name of God and your truest, deepest identity as a child of God. I AM has no limitations and can have, do, or become ANYTHING.

You are in no way inferior to any great spiritual master. You are equally divine, just as powerful, and can perform the same feats if you could only overcome the energetic friction caused by your doubts and lack of belief. Remember what Jesus said: When you go to the Father (your inner sense of I AM or pure being), you will "do the works I have been doing, and…will do even greater things than these". But fret not. Thankfully, you can obtain incredible results in health, wealth, love, and other domains of your life even if you don't have the same degree of perfect faith as a Buddha or a Jesus. You can gradually build your faith in your unlimited creative power. We will now discuss how to do this.

* * * * * * * * * *

Chapter 4: Master Beliefs and Heart Harmony

The 3 Paramorphing Master Beliefs

If a person had perfect faith, he could order the seas to part, and they would instantly obey him just as they did for Moses or Krishna. Perfect faith can move mountains, close up mile-wide canyons, turn brass into hold, instantly heal malignant tumors, and even create new universes in a split-second.

This is the power of perfect faith: It claims a desired PRL with absolute, unwavering conviction and simply declares that the new PRL is here, knowing all things are possible with God.

Of course, on Earth, perfect faith is almost impossible to find except in the case of enlightened masters such as Krishna, Jesus, Rama, and Sai Baba of Shirdi. Why do saints and perfect wizards have the ability to instantly materialize any PRL? For the simple reason that they have completely died to their limited human mind (as human beings) and fully and deeply know that they are God playing the role of a human. Their individual mind has permanently dipped into the heart zone where one is tethered to the divine mind of God, which has access to all PRLs. Yet, ironically, because the heart zone is capable of materializing any PRL but does not have preferences or desires, enlightened masters will typically have no desires other than to fulfill the wishes and desires of those coming to them and requesting their help.

For the 99.9999% of humans on earth who are not at this level, faith exists alongside the force of friction, which delays and impedes new PRLs from materializing into physical reality. Friction clogs the machine of creation.

This master set of Paramorphing beliefs will remove massive amounts of friction in almost any domain, whether it be wealth, health, love, or relationships. It is VITAL to internalize this master set of Paramorphing beliefs before going forward. Consider these beliefs to be a "reset of your internal operating system", to use an analogy from the world of computers. If your core operating system is flawed or outdated, running other programs on top of it becomes frustratingly hard, slow, and nearly impossible. In the same way that an updated and efficient operating system is necessary to run modern computer programs and apps, your internal operating system needs to first be updated before you can easily morph to your desired PRL.

The 3 Paramorphing Master Beliefs:

1. I am a child of God, made in the image of the Creator who flows through me. The Creator's name is I AM, so everything I could desire exists. This literally means that all possibilities are available to me if I choose them. I am the sole architect, controller, and decider of my fate, for this is my divine right as a child of God. I accept responsibility for everything in my life now and recognize that I have now been vested with the power and knowledge to perfectly modify and transform my life.

2. God has already created all PRLs, meaning that I do not have to try, strive, or struggle for anything. The divine Eternal Cosmic Library of infinite possibilities was given to me as a gift, and I am inherently worthy of having anything and everything I want. My limited human mind may have no idea how to bring a PRL into physical reality, but that's perfectly fine because that's not its job. The job of my mind is to merely choose and feel that my new PRL is already mine. My invisible higher self, which I access through my heart zone, knows how to bring anything I desire into physical reality.

3. I am doing everything perfectly. As soon as I firmly decide that a PRL is mine, all my actions and all circumstances around me begin unfolding perfectly toward bringing about my newly chosen PRL. It doesn't matter what I do or don't do, or whether

circumstances around me appear favorable or unfavorable: My higher self knows the most efficient route and is orchestrating events perfectly in time and space to bring about my desire.

These 3 foundational Paramorphing beliefs are so important in overcoming friction that I humbly advise people to meditate on them for at least 15 minutes a day. They are so powerful that they can even replace current meditation practices that you might have. They will dissolve both specific frictions you might have stemming from limited beliefs and insecurities in particular domains, as well as more general friction that humans have, as a group, in doubting they can fully shape and control their destiny. The parable of the Pearl of Great Price says that "the kingdom of heaven is like a merchant seeking beautiful pearls, who, when he had found one pearl of great price, went and sold all that he had and bought it". What is this kingdom of heaven? It is nothing but your inner sense of I AM, the formless consciousness within you that immediately turns into whatever form and PRL you truly feel you are. Once you find it, know that you and you alone are the cause of your entire reality. There is no person, event, or circumstance "out there" who has a say in how your life experience turns out unless you relinquish your inner authority.

The divine printer of creation takes any PRL fed into it and claimed, and perfectly spits it out into physical reality. It does not choose, morally judge, condemn, or play favorites. This is crucial to note. There is no "external power" withholding your desires from you or determining if you're worthy. IT IS ONLY YOU, AND IT HAS ALWAYS BEEN ONLY YOU. Faith is the perfect love that arises from recognizing that the Creator has already given you everything, including PRLs in which you already have everything you desire. Faith is centered in the heart. Friction is the force of perfect fear, doubting whether your desired PRL is possible for you to have. Friction is centered in the head, the logical and conscious thinking mind. Friction is the bottleneck that clogs the divine printer of creation from turning imagined PRLs into physical reality.

With perfect faith, one would instantly glide into the desired reality. With perfect fear, one would forever be stuck and unable to make any changes. Thus, the interplay of these two forces is the reason why God's language of creation is called **Paramorphing (Parallel Reality Layer Morphing)**. Your physical reality gradually morphs to match the PRL that you have faithfully and feelingly declared yourself to be in imagination and internally embody as your self-concept. The higher your ratio of faith to fear, the more quickly and smoothly your new PRL comes into physical realization. With perfect faith, there are absolutely no limits to what you can experience. None whatsoever.

Your Heart's Harmonic Signature

There is one other vitally important factor to note: Your heart's unique harmonic signature. It is, indeed, possible to be or have anything because with the force of faith, all PRLs can be channeled into physical reality. However, each person will have a unique set of absolutely burning and compelling desires that they wish to have above all else. These are the things that you want most in life, above everything else, and don't have to think twice about. In Paramorphing, this is called the heart's Harmonic Signature, the characteristic energy of your truest and most genuine self. Everyone intrinsically knows what they truly want; however, societal and cultural programming stifles and smothers the heart's burning fire, pushing people to settle for less. Perhaps you were born to parents who lamented nonstop that wealth is difficult to come by and that fame and riches are for only a select few, a group which they definitely professed they were not and would never be a part of. You may have a deep and burning desire to start a world-changing business, own a custom-outfitted private jet, achieve record-setting athletic glory as a star quarterback, top the Billboard 100 as a Grammy-winning guitarist who sells out Shea Stadium, or merge with God and master astral travelling while attaining Buddhahood.

Any possibility, if it can be imagined, can be crystallized into physical reality. Yet, when moving to the PRLs associated with your soul's harmonic signature, you may face tremendous friction from others around you who expect you to conform to socially established standards around acceptable behavior. They may even advise you to even abandon your wishes and pursue more "realistic" outcomes instead of "being delusional". Earth offers a unique challenge for the soul in learning how to ignore and overcome such frictional forces and develop the courage to pursue your heart's Harmonic Signature. The beauty of your unique Harmonic Signature is that the overwhelming love you have for your truest desires and deepest wishes will absolutely obliterate friction. Your Harmonic Signature is the most authentic version of you and your strongest desires represent how God, the creator, wishes to experience himself through you! Your burning desires are already yours and a gift from God, if you could only have the courage to say YES to them. When you recognize your heart's Harmonic Signature, you will find that nothing can stop you and that every possible obstacle will magically melt away. If there is physical work involved in the realization of your desire, such as training for an athletic contest or working on an investment deck to raise money for your business, you will surprisingly find that the physical work energizes you instead of draining you.

Remember, each person has a singular harmonic signature. Pursuing someone else's goals or Harmonic Signature leads to burnout, depression, disappointment, and lack of fulfillment. Society and cultural norms try to impose a uniform, cookie-cutter, "cog-in-the-machine" Harmonic Signature on individuals, which kills the soul's joy and explains why most people despise and barely tolerate the work they do. If they had the courage to truly examine their heart's Harmonic Signature and accept this into their lives, regardless of what society imposes on them, they would find magical pathways opening up that crystallize their wishes into reality. The heart is connected to the divine mind of God, the Eternal

Cosmic Library of infinite PRLs. There is quite literally NOTHING that is beyond your reach if you say yes to your Harmonic Signature and accept who you are instead of running away from your wishes from doubt or fear. Why settle and live a quiet life of despair and desperation when infinity is at your fingertips? Your heart zone has access to ALL PRLs.

Your heart's Harmonic Signature also includes the type of work you do in the physical world and the vocation, hobbies, and interests you pursue. Keep in mind that heeding your heart's Harmonic Signature is the ONLY way to find deep fulfillment, joy, and meaning in your life. You can have 100 million followers on social media or billions, even trillions of dollars, but if you are not following your heart's Harmonic Signature, your soul will feel restless, incomplete, and dissatisfied. The Buddha was born Siddhartha Gautama, a prince who grew up in absolute luxury surrounded by vast riches, immense privileges, and a line of beautiful women throwing themselves at him. Yet, none of these pleasures satisfied his heart's Harmonic Signature, which was to realize his oneness with God and become a spiritual luminary and benchmark for mankind. The Buddha demonstrated absolute courage and conviction in throwing away a life most would dream of, but he knew at the core of his being that his heart's Harmonic Signature was worth more than all the riches in the world combined. And thanks to his unswerving conviction, to this day, his name is remembered, glorified, and celebrated all over the world.

Your Harmonic signature, of course, does not need to be the same as the Buddha's. Only you can know what it is. Test this for yourself, right now, with absolute honesty. You know, in the deepest core of your being, what your heart's fondest and deepest aspirations are. No one has to tell you what your truest calling is. Now imagine yourself near the end of your life, having accomplished immense success in multiple domains, but WITHOUT having achieved your heart's Harmonic Signature. Do you feel whole, peaceful, and content? The answer will be a resounding NO. Your heart's Harmonic Signature is a message from your all-knowing and all-wise higher self (God) telling you exactly what you should be pursuing and focusing on in this current lifetime.

When you have the courage to trust and follow your heart's Harmonic Signature, regardless of the objections or doubts of your limited conscious mind, you will find miraculous pathways lighting up and effortlessly taking you to PRLs in which ALL your desires are effortlessly fulfilled. When you follow your heart's Harmonic Signature, you are activating the infinite power of the heart zone, which starts flooding your entire life with happiness and harmony. Having activated the divine magnetic power of the heart zone, which is tethered to the infinite power of God, you will find that people, desires, objects, and achievements start chasing YOU, rather than the other way around.

We will now examine the 7 frictional forces that hinder people from Paramorphing to their desired PRLs, as well as how to mitigate them. Remember that everything you perceive in your reality is merely a second-order effect of your beliefs. As such, the single most powerful Paramorphing process is to clearly believe in your truest identity as a child of God, already having and being all that is. Know that you are never creating something outside of you, but merely choosing to bring into focus a PRL that is ALREADY CONTAINED within you, for you are a ray of the infinite Creator.

* * * * * * * * * *

Chapter 5: The 7 Flavors of Friction

Factor 1: Doubt and Delusion

The first and perhaps most fundamental frictional force that clogs the divine printer of creation, is doubt and delusion. The veil of amnesia required for entering Earth, one of the densest realms, obscures every soul that enters this planet. When you come to Earth, you forget your innate divine glory as an infinite child of God. It is hard for some to accept that a higher power such as God even exists. It can also be hard to accept you are a child of this omnipotent Creator. It is harder to accept that you have created and chosen your entire life experience, every single bit of it. It is harder still to have faith that you have access to an Eternal Cosmic Library, the divine mind of God, and can literally have whatever your heart desires. And it is perhaps hardest of all to realize that you are not only a child of God or a divine soul, but God himself; the SUPREME divine creator, ALL THAT IS, limiting yourself so you can enjoy and experience your infinitude in an infinite number of ways.

At best, most humans believe that their circumstances in life are determined by some combination of genetics (factors beyond their control), the family they were born into, actions they take in the physical world, and luck. The fact that you can actually change EVERYTHING might seem fanciful at best and dangerously delusional at worst, but this is only because of the veil of amnesia you cloaked over yourself when you came to Earth. Paramorphing awakens you. You are GOD and you have picked every circumstance in your life, including the so-called "factors you had no control over", and even set up specific experiences you wanted to encounter during your present lifetime such as the family you would be born in. You agreed to all these constraints so that you, God, could have a richly realistic experience of one specific PRL as a human being, on planet Earth, in a particular timeframe.

Why has Paramorphing found its way into your hands at this specific time? Perhaps you planned to awaken at a certain time during your current life, and this book is the means of facilitating that awakening. Or perhaps you have searched for a way to obtain your desires or change your life. Either way, there is no excuse to remain asleep in the dream, now that you have the holy grail.

Yes, your waking life is a dream. Think about the dreams you have at night. You are plunged into various scenarios, environments, and challenges, and deal with other people. You endure intensely realistic emotions and highs and lows, whether you have sweet dreams or nightmares. For instance, you might dream about being chased by a cheetah in a forest or enjoying a party with friends in the city. However, when you wake up in the morning, you realize that there is no city, forest, party, cheetah, or friends. The entire dream was a projection that came from WITHIN YOU. It all happened inside you.

Ironically, though, while you were ensconced in the dream, you were not aware that all the objects and people you saw were projections created by you. You took them to be separate "others" and saw yourself as a separate being in an external environment, not realizing that everything you perceived to be **external** was merely a projection of your own **internal** consciousness.

Paramorphing explains how dreams truly function. Your dreams are not false. They are REAL PRLs that your mind experiences while you are sleeping. It doesn't matter how fanciful your dreams may appear to be at night; they are imaginative experiences of your mind, and remember, if you can imagine it, it exists in the Eternal Cosmic Library of God's divine mind and can be brought into physical experience. When you dream, your heart zone can quite literally take you into any PRL without the doubts or limiting beliefs of your conscious mind. For example, in a dream, you can fly, make your body bioluminescent, or swallow an entire lake. The only reason you find these feats impossible while you are awake is because your conscious mind has an absolute conviction in limits and constraints such as the laws of physics. In reality, natural laws such as gravity are not objective truths but merely very strong core beliefs.

To the awakened sage or wizard, the world you see while you are awake is fundamentally no different than a dream, except for the fact that your waking world appears consistent and predictable each morning because it contains the added element of memory. As such, you wake up each morning "remembering" your name, identity in the world of form, profession, family, and trillions of other details that lend a sense of solidity to this illusion. This massive process occurs in a split-second as your mind rises from your heart zone, where it rests in deep sleep inside the Eternal Cosmic Library of God, to the head zone, where it rises to project your PRL, thereby creating the world you experience as your waking reality. Without your sense of memory, the world you witness when you wake up in the morning would be as chaotic, seemingly new, and confusing as a dream you had at night.

All this might be too much for the human mind to process. Yes, indeed, it can be overwhelming to realize that there is no world outside of you and that everyone and everything you see is just a projection of your own mind. So how does one resolve this doubt?

There are only two paths. You can either take the truths of Paramorphing at face value, blindly trust and apply them, get results, and then gradually and experientially know that you are, indeed, the sole creator of your entire reality. Or you can pursue the more intense route of self-inquiry, which will reveal the glorious nature of your being to you, but it is not for the faint of heart. As Jesus boldly declares in the Gospel of Thomas, "Let one who seeks not stop seeking until that person finds; and upon finding, the person will be disturbed; and being disturbed, will be astounded; and will reign over the entirety". Why will seeking make a person disturbed then astounded? For the simple but profound reason that seeking who you truly are will lead to the answer that you are God in human form, the sole creator of your perceived reality, and the master of your destiny. The entire world that you took to be a separate entity outside of you will be revealed as your own mental movie, a movie in which you are the actor, author, producer, and director! You are creating all of it, here and now. Wonderful results are produced when a person combines both paths. We will now discuss a basic template for pursuing self-inquiry, and cover practical application techniques for Paramorphing in the next chapter.

Self-inquiry consists of simply asking yourself who you really are. You peel back the layers of your reality, one by one, seeing what is consistent, eternal, and true no matter what. There is no one-size-fits-all process here. Some people awaken to the truth of their eternal formless God-identity (I AM) instantly while others go through a more gradual process. The root of self-inquiry is absolute stillness, for it is in stillness that you become aware of your deepest and truest identity as pure consciousness. The Biblical writer of Psalm 46 captured it perfectly: "Be still and know I AM God".

You can start by asking if you exist without your physical body. Well, clearly, you can. You definitely exist in your dreams, and feel yourself to have a solid physical body, though it is obviously not the body you feel while you are awake. You may dream of being in a younger version of your body, such as oversleeping your alarm and being late for school even though that was decades ago. You may even experience dreams as other creatures. One great Zen master had a dream of being a butterfly in a garden, and upon waking the next morning wondered if he was a human dreaming of being a butterfly or a butterfly dreaming of being a human! Clearly, your consciousness remains independent and unchanged even when you move through different bodies, like a driver switching from one car to another.

The next step would be to see if you exist without your mind. Do you? Observe yourself during deep dreamless sleep. During deep sleep, you clearly exist, though you have no conception of yourself as a creature with a specific form. You don't disappear or dissolve into nothingness while you are deep asleep. You simply wake up the next morning with a rejuvenated sense of peace and calm. If you are attentive to the precious moments immediately after you wake up, before your sense of bodily identity kicks back in, you will clearly know and feel that you are actually pure, intangible, and eternal consciousness, or I AM. This is your real identity as a child of God, an unlimited wave of pure consciousness that can become anything.

Another means of self-inquiry is to ask what part of you has remained constant, from the day you were born to the present day. Your body grew rapidly, your thoughts changed, your intelligence level changed, and the people and environments around you changed, but there was only **one** thing that ALWAYS remained consistent: Your sense of I AM, or pure being, unaffected by any temporary forms that arose within it. It is the one and only thing you can never lose because it is your infinite and perpetual God-self.

Your pure consciousness of being, or I AM, is your higher self, the divine eternal field of God that contains PRL templates for any and every possible reality. While I have illustrated a hypothetical self-inquiry process above, please note that merely reading my words will do absolutely nothing for you. You cannot get to the root of your being by cognitively trying to understand it. You must **experientially** marinate on these words and ceaselessly ask yourself who you truly are, until you TANGIBLY know and feel, without a doubt, that you are the pure consciousness of God, the ultimate reality that is beyond time and space and always IS. God never was, and God never will be. **GOD SIMPLY IS**. Time, space, and the universe all require God; but God needs none of them. God is self-luminous, independent, and omnipotent, and YOU ARE THIS GOD!

Once you start glimpsing this truth, start observing everything that has transpired in your life, ranging from experiences you found to be positive to those you found to be negative, and everything in between. This can be painful, for you will be forced to ruthlessly strip apart your own delusions and conceptions of yourself, others, and the world you have experienced all your life, but the rewards are priceless. **You will see that you have created your entire reality through your mind, specifically your thoughts, assumptions, and beliefs.** For example, if there's a certain individual you have not gotten along with or who seems to not like you, take a close look at your beliefs and assumptions about that person. If your financial situation is not to your liking, examine your deepest beliefs about money, your financial self-concept, and whether you truly feel you are worthy of enjoying wealth. If you are utterly and totally honest in your assessment, you will realize that every output in your reality was created by your imaginative input. You, in other words, have consciously or unconsciously created your current PRL: ALL OF IT, every bit of it.

Now that you understand Paramorphing, the most wonderful news is that you can completely transform your entire life. Your conception of who you are, and who you define and truly feel yourself to be, will override and reverse all the thoughts, assumptions, and prior beliefs that created your currently experienced PRL. BEING takes precedence over thinking, acting, doing, feeling, and emoting. BEING is the primary cause of all reality. When you embody a new PRL by living it here and now, with total commitment and faith, it MUST crystallize into physical reality. Jesus's original instructions in the Book of John reveal this clearly and explicitly: "All things that you ask straightly and directly from inside my name you shall be given. So far you have not done this. Ask without hidden motives and be surrounded by your answer. Be enveloped by what you desire, that your gladness be full". What is the name Jesus speaks of? Jesus tells us he is one with the Father or God. The name of God is "I AM". In other words,

Jesus is telling us that we can have anything, absolutely ALL THINGS if we genuinely embody the corresponding PRL here and now, surrounding ourselves with the joy and satisfaction of already having whatever we desire. Everything already belongs to you.

The **Paramorphing Pyramid** demonstrates this in detail. There are 4 levels or "levers" a person can manipulate to morph from one PRL to another. The higher the level, the more potent it is in facilitating a PRL shift.

The Paramorphing Pyramid

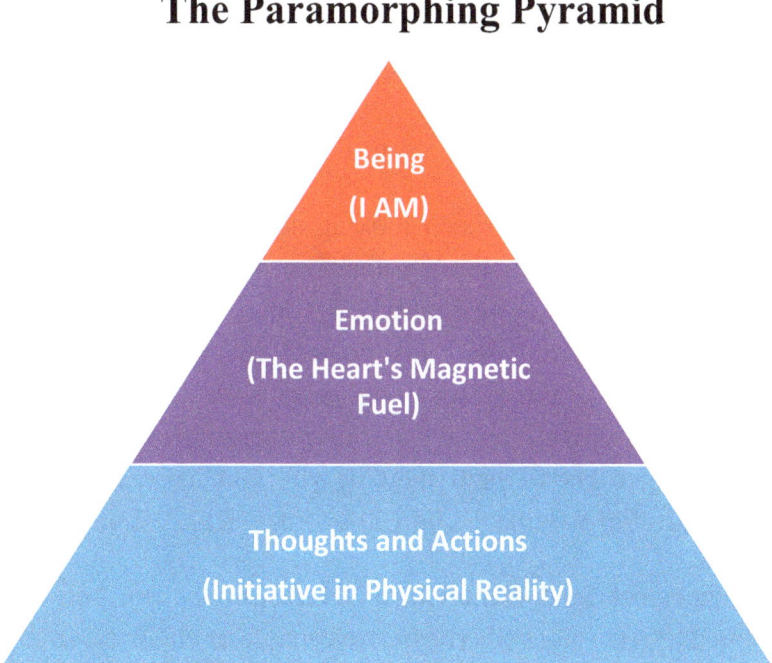

The highest level of the Paramorphing Pyramid is the feeling of I AM and WHO you are conscious of **BEING**. This is why Jesus states "I am the vine; you are the branches. If you remain in me and I in you, you will bear much fruit; apart from me you can do nothing". Your I AMness, or who you are conscious of being, is the most fundamental determinant of your reality. The fruits you bear are directly congruent with who you deeply feel you are. You cannot bear fruits of health, wealth, joy, and fortune if you identify as a person who is sick, poor, miserable, and needs to struggle to get things in life. **Who do you say and truly feel you are?** This is by far the most powerful layer of Paramorphing, for when you truly feel that you are in your desired PRL, no matter what your current PRL is showing, your physical circumstances have no choice BUT to gradually morph you into your desired reality. It is God's divine law, and there are no exceptions. The beauty is once you have locked yourself in the conviction of **BEING** your new PRL, your emotions, thoughts, and actions naturally flow from this new PRL identity and help to rapidly crystallize your desired PRL into physical reality. The divine creative printer, remember, does not play favorites. It simply and precisely spits out what you feed into it, namely WHO and WHAT you are conscious of being, and serves this up as your experience of physical reality.

What happens if you keep looking at your current PRL with continued despair, complaining about it, and taking it to be an objective and unchanging reality? By doing this, what you are effectively saying is I AM my present (undesired) PRL. And because you continue identifying with your current physical circumstances as who you are, the divine printer of creation will have no choice but to keep showing you your current undesired reality instead of Paramorphing you into new and desirable PRLs.

At the most fundamental level, there is only one belief that matters: Do you truly believe you are capable of choosing your life circumstances and do you believe that you are actually in total control over your life? The divine printer of creation never judges and there is only one absolute law it follows: It spits out precisely what you are conscious of being. If you believe you are NOT capable of moving to your desired reality and that life is a struggle and unpredictably chaotic affair, you will be choosing and breathing life into a PRL in which life is, indeed, a struggle and you cannot easily move to new PRLs.

The divine law of Paramorphing is always working whether one is conscious of it or not: Each and every moment, you are broadcasting your entire world from your mind, exclusively based on the PRL you have chosen to identify as. There is no fixed past or future: Each and every nanosecond, you are broadcasting your entire life experience from the eternal NOW. You are shifting through trillions of PRLs each second, though they are so similar that your physical reality appears coherent, solid, and objective. It is a grand illusion. In fact, everything is up for grabs, so to speak, and your entire reality is pulsating with infinite potential and changing nanosecond by nanosecond. The key to directing this infinite flow of energy is your I AM center of awareness, which can transform anything and everything around you.

After conducting self-inquiry and realizing you are the pure, formless God-consciousness that has access to ALL POSSIBLE PRLs, the second step to overcoming the friction associated with doubt is to start proving the law Paramorphing to yourself. Each person will have domains of Paramorphing that they feel less friction toward. For instance, one person might find it easy to make more money and shift to a PRL in which he gets a salary bonus as he feels confident, worthy, and deserving in the domain of career success, yet find it difficult to believe he could move to the PRL in which he is happily married due to his lackluster beliefs regarding relationships. Another person might easily attract their dream partner yet feel great friction toward Paramorphing into a reality in which they earn more, due to childhood trauma stemming from poor money beliefs while growing up in a family with debt.

Start with a domain where you have a substantial amount of self-belief and worthiness, and move with conviction into a newly desired PRL. Once you prove Paramorphing in one domain, you can branch out into other domains, realizing that in God's eyes, all domains are equal. There is no judgment of "superior" or "inferior" in the divine mind. The divine mind of God which contains the Eternal Cosmic Library of all PRLs was given to you as a GIFT.

Jesus reminded us of this great gift that has been given to us freely: "Fear not, little flock; for it is your Father's good pleasure to give you the kingdom". Remember the Paramorphing master beliefs: You do not need to strive or prove your worthiness. You are not here to "learn lessons" or "suffer" unless you choose to believe this. You are a DIVINE CHILD OF GOD and a window through which God, the infinite Creator, enjoys himself through experience. The entire Eternal Cosmic Library of infinite PRLs, or kingdom of heaven, has already been given to you. Then, does it make any sense to struggle to prove your worthiness? Deep down, your heart already knows the answer. Absolutely not! You are INFINITELY worthy.

BEING comes first. It is the most important part of Paramorphing and the top layer of the Paramorphing Pyramid. All forms of feeling, thinking, doing, and acting are downstream effects or secondary causes that flow from the primary cause of being. Humanity has forgotten this, which is a major reason why people find it difficult or impossible to Paramorph to their new desired PRLs. They act, struggle, and wrestle with the world without changing their conception of who they are! Even highly intelligent philosophers have made this grave error. Descartes, for example, famously declared "I think, therefore I am". This is an inversion of Paramorphing. The correct statement according to divine law would be "I AM, therefore I think (and act, feel, do, and have)". I AM God himself, the foundational cause and source of ALL realities.

Now that we have established that the MOST important factor is your inner conviction of who you truly feel to be, we can address the remaining layers of the Paramorphing Pyramid.

The bottom layer of the Paramorphing Pyramid is thoughts and actions, the initiatives you take in the physical world toward a newly desired PRL. If you are not conscious of already BEING in your desired PRL, your actions will amount to nothing. They may seem to be perfect on paper, even what society would deem as logical toward the realization of a desire, but if you do not identify as already being the person who resides in your desired PRL, your actions will take you nowhere. You will keep going in circles, wondering why tremendous effort and strain yield such poor results. For example, suppose a tennis player wishes to enter the top 10 of the world rankings. This is his desired PRL. He can train, practice, and exert as much effort as he wants, but internally, if he does not identify as and feel himself to already be a top 10 player, his efforts will absolutely be in vain. The same is true for thoughts. A person can repeat affirmations, prayers, mantras, and positive motivational dialogues all day long, but if they are recited from the standpoint of someone who does NOT already have a particular desire, that desire will never come to fruition until the person changes his self-concept to be "I am already in my new PRL". The beauty here is that when someone firmly identifies INTERNALLY as the person who already resides in a certain PRL, she will automatically be internally guided to take the appropriate actions and think the correct thoughts that move her toward the crystallization of that PRL into physical reality. Everything she does, or doesn't do, will be correct and blessed with the Midas Touch of the entire universe conspiring to make her intended PRL a physical reality. God does not judge or question your desires. When you accept a PRL as your identity, with conviction, it is willed into solid reality.

Therefore, the top layer of the Paramorphing Pyramid is I AM X, with X being whatever PRL a person wishes to occupy, and the bottom layer is thoughts and actions taken in the physical world. One question remains. What is the invisible energetic force that takes a person's imagined PRL template and converts it into physically experienced reality? This infinitely powerful electromagnetic force is LOVING CONVICTION, and it stems from the heart zone where all PRL templates exist in latent potential until they are called into physical reality. The heart zone's energy is pure, unconditional, and absolute love, which never judges but simply materializes whatever is asked of it. It is important to note that love is both infinitely humble and infinitely powerful; it asks for nothing but is capable of materializing everything.

The heart's energy of pure and unconditionally **loving conviction** constitutes your truest and deepest nature. Gratitude, contentment, peace, joy, relief, and confidence are sub-frequencies or variants of the heart's Godly energy. When a person believes he has already received his new PRL HERE and NOW, and mentally resides in his new PRL, he will feel one of these sub-frequencies or a combination of them. These sub-frequencies, borne of the heart's infinitely powerful energy of love, are the secret magnetic forces that propel you toward your desired PRL. For instance, a person who desires a new car, as we will discuss in the Practical Application of Paramorphing chapter, might mentally envision himself driving his new car by draping that "reality skin" over whatever car he drives currently. If he does this truly and authentically, he will automatically feel a sense of gratitude, joy, relief, contentment, or some combination of these sub-frequencies. It is important to NOT force a particular sub-frequency but to naturally embrace whichever one(s) emerge as a result of your internal visualization. For example, one person might be filled with a sense of joy and cheer when imagining that they are already happily married to their perfect life partner. Another person might feel a deep sense of relief and calmness, knowing that they no longer have to spend time searching for a life partner. Still, another person might be filled with an intangible sense of energy and purpose, knowing that they can now buy a home or do any number of things they had planned to do after getting married. The key is to simply embody your desired PRL and then let your heart zone naturally produce a corresponding sub-frequency. The one thing all these sub-frequencies share in common is that they are felt in the heart. This is why people value things that are "heartfelt", whether they are apologies, declarations of love, or pleas. The heart zone's energy is connected to the Eternal Cosmic Library and God's infinite power, so when the heart is appropriately invoked, all things truly become possible. **All things.**

Factor 2: Pedestalization of the Desired PRL

The divine printer of creation is powered by faith and slowed by friction. These are the only two forces that govern Paramorphing. One of the most powerful sources of friction, one that quite literally chokes the divine printer of creation, is pedestalizing your desired PRL and desperately craving it while simultaneously feeling that you are unworthy of attaining it. In extreme cases, a person might even feel that his life is just "not worth living" without the pedestalized object or person. For example, a man might pedestalize a particular romantic partner, dreaming of a life with her and pining for the day he is with her, while bitterly despising his current PRL in which he is not with her. Others might despise their current PRL in which they are poor, pining desperately for a desired PRL in which they are finally rich, all the while deeply believing they are not worthy of such opulence. Pedestalization feels deeply painful and hopelessly agonizing.

Remember, all desires are divine and stem from the urge of the Creator to know himself in totality. Thus, desire is not wrong, evil, sinful, or "bad". However, desperation in WANTING a desire, rather than simply claiming it and knowing you already HAVE it within you, causes tremendous friction and prevents you from Paramorphing to your desired new PRL.

The divine printer can only reflect what you feed into it. WANTING or CRAVING a particular new PRL, which you deem as especially alluring, only means one thing to the divine printer: That you are conscious of NOT HAVING IT. And if you are not conscious of having it in your imagination, physical reality most certainly cannot produce the PRL of you having that object or experience. The act of chasing anything, including a desired PRL, only repels it further from you. If your craving and desperation are strong enough, you can be obsessed and consumed by the notion of WANTING your new PRL, yet no amount of this desperation will get you an inch closer to having your desired PRL crystallize into your physical reality.

Does this appear cruel? Only from the standpoint of the limited human mind. From the standpoint of God's divine mind and urge to know himself, it makes perfect sense. The goal and objective of creation for God is to know himself and to realize HE IS EVERYTHING. God doesn't crave or beg. God CLAIMS and APPROPRIATES any particular reality.

When you pedestalize a person, object, or experience, what you are effectively doing is declaring yourself UNWORTHY of having it. You are also declaring that you do not already contain the desired PRL within yourself. Your heart zone is connected to the Eternal Cosmic Library of infinite PRLs, so pedestalization is equivalent to you feeling that you CANNOT access your desired PRL or that it is somehow "too good" for you.

Can anything be "too good" for God? Obviously not. The supreme creator is the LORD and OWNER of all PRLs, and you are a child of this infinite power. The most beautiful romantic partner or trillions of dollars are nothing before the glory and majesty of the Creator, I AM, who is the only permanent reality and the sole reality that sustains all PRLs. Pedestalization is only possible when you forget your true nature as a child of God equipped with infinite potential.

Stop pedestalizing people, objects, and experiences, and start pedestalizing your inner I AM, the pure consciousness within you that links you to your higher God-self. There is ALREADY a PRL in which you have whatever you desire, so desperately craving for it makes no sense! Secure this PRL in your imagination. If you truly feel that you are already in the PRL where you have and enjoy whatever you used to pedestalize, it must appear in your reality.

You can be grateful for something you have, but you cannot crave it. Just think of the objects you currently own in your physical reality, such as the car you drive. You might appreciate it, and that is wonderful. You may even be proud of it. But you certainly would not pedestalize it or think of it as "being too good for you". You could only pedestalize something you don't have or feel that you could not have. This is why people pedestalize luxury brands. And, of course, those who pedestalize luxury and feel it to be out of reach will never have it in their lives; they can never move to the PRL of having these objects as they do not have a natural sense of ease in having them. Your physical reality will only consist of things you feel you naturally have and deserve to have.

The poor man pedestalizes luxury vehicles. The rich man, who owns the luxury vehicle, feels as comfortable in the luxury vehicle as the poor man does in his 20-year-old rundown minivan. There is inherently nothing better about the PRL of wealth versus the PRL of poverty, for they are both equal in God's eyes. Each person is merely attracting to himself precisely the objects that correspond to what he naturally feels at ease with having. The same is true of a man who pedestalizes a particular woman, racking himself with depression and pining for the day he is married to her. Of course, that day will never come. On the other hand, if he realizes that there is already an existing PRL in which he is married to her, and feels the natural state of being married to her, which includes being aware of her strengths and weaknesses, and her flawed humanity, he will move to the PRL in which he is with her. **You are already inherently worthy of everything that you desire.**

Pedestalize God, and know that your inner sense of I AM is worth more than everything in the entire universe. Once you do this, pedestalization will die in your life and the divine printer of creation will rapidly print your desired PRL.

Decide that you already have the things you desire, and also realize that even without having those things physically, you are always I AM, the infinite creator who transcends people, places, objects, and the whole universe.

To strongly desire something means that there is already a PRL, a very close PRL, in which you possess that very thing. Rejoice! Desire is a clear sign and indicator from God showing you the experiences you could have if you choose them. Dwell on having that PRL, consume yourself with it, and cremate your cravings and longings, for you already have that which you formerly desired.

Cremation precedes creation. Cremate your low self-image and feelings of unworthiness, rise anew like a divine phoenix, and crystallize your desired PRL by realizing you are inherently worthy of ALL THAT IS as a divine child of God. This doesn't mean you need to dread negative thoughts and feelings that may initially arise. Simply observe them neutrally, the way you would notice clouds in the sky. Then, gently but firmly reaffirm your newly chosen identity and PRL of already having whatever you formerly desired.

Factor 3: Aversion to the Existing PRL

In order for a new PRL to crystallize as your physical reality, the old or current PRL that you experience must dissolve, obviously. However, obsessing or excessively complaining about your current PRL clogs the divine printer of creation. Bitter resistance toward your current PRL generates intense friction that prevents the current PRL from exiting your reality.

Remember: Your mentally imagined concept of who you are, your deeply felt sense of I AMness, is the PRL template that eventually crystallizes into your experienced physical reality. When you think about your present circumstances and appearances with great irritation, you are effectively telling the divine printer of creation, "this current set of undesired circumstances is who I AM!". By excessively dwelling on the current PRL, you are implicitly accepting it as your identity and giving it power over you, rather than recognizing it as a stale reflection of your FORMER state of being. When you judge, complain, attack, and try to coerce your present reality, it is like trying to loosen yourself from the jaws of a tiger by pulling away harder and harder. The more desperately you try to escape, the more deeply the tiger's inwardly curved teeth sink into your flesh, trapping you even more.

The old parable of the sun and the wind is a perfect demonstration of how to avoid the Paramorphing pitfall of fighting your currently existing PRL. The sun and the wind both saw a man wearing a heavy coat and challenged each other to see who could get the man to remove his coat. The wind, deciding to pursue the path of coercive force, blew with great force at the man, but the harder it blew, the more tightly the man gripped onto his coat to survive the cold gales. The wind gave up, at which point the sun had its turn. The sun did nothing but simply smile, relaxing into BEING and flooding the atmosphere with its gentle warmth, without any active attempt to force the man to do anything. And surely enough, the man automatically realized he didn't need a coat anymore in the warm weather, and he decided to take his coat off.

The wind attempted to battle the present PRL with coercion. The sun simply let the present PRL fade away. Your attention is a precious and limited resource that can only claim ONE PRL AT A TIME. You can either be in your desired new PRL mentally, knowing that the current PRL is merely an old reflection that will fade away, or you can be stuck in the current PRL, recreating that as your physical reality as you continue to dwell on it with frustration and irritation.

The earth realm is unique because it forces souls to learn a degree of patience, persistence, and conviction that they cannot learn in other realms. In the astral heavens, for instance, simply choosing a new PRL causes it to come into physical existence immediately or with a very short time lag. On earth, the parameters of time and space are relatively dense so certain PRLs may take days, weeks, months, or even years to come to fruition, but the law of Paramorphing is certain. Whatever you honestly claim and feel yourself to be MUST eventually morph into your experienced physical reality. And if you feel something is time-sensitive, such as getting enough money to pay off a debt or finding a life partner while you are biologically healthy enough to have kids, do not create friction by worrying about whether it will show up too late in your life. God is all-knowing and cannot be mocked, for as the Book of Isaiah assures, "before they call, I will answer; and while they are yet speaking, I will hear". Your new PRL will harden into physical reality at a perfect time. Simply persist in being it NOW.

Humans on earth are instructed, as children, to see the physical world as the "true" reality and their mental conceptions and imagination as "just fantasy" or "make-believe". This is yet another challenge of undergoing the amnesic veil to enter Earth. Most humans entirely forget that imaginative self-concept, or who you feelingly declare as I AM, is the true CAUSAL reality, and the physical world you see is merely a PRL that crystallized into existence because you first EMBODIED IT MENTALLY. It is the end product. If you were making soup, for instance, and it turned out to be too spicy, would you try to "lessen" the spiciness of the completed product? It would lead to poor results at best and inedible soup at worst. Rather, the wise approach would be to remake the soup with a different recipe that uses fewer chilies, rather than worrying about or obsessing over the currently made soup which is spicy and unpalatable.

Do not worry about your present PRL that shows up as physical reality. Realize it to be the product of your prior beliefs and the old imaginative PRL you identified with, consciously or unconsciously. Then, rejoice by realizing that if you could create misery in your life, you can just as easily create happiness.

Do not worry about how the old PRL gets displaced and replaced by the new PRL. Forget about the old PRL, and do not identify with it anymore, for doing so will cause the divine printer of creation to keep "reprinting" the old PRL template into physical existence. The infinite intelligence of God knows how to seamlessly and perfectly transition you from the old PRL to the new PRL.

All you must do is to faithfully persist in the new PRL no matter what, without looking to the external world to confirm your change, and without being discouraged by the time it takes for your new PRL to crystallize within the time-space fabric of the earth realm. The price you pay for any desired PRL is your willingness to faithfully know you have it EVEN BEFORE there is a shred of evidence in physical reality to support your new identity. The Book of 2 Kings captures this Paramorphing concept perfectly. When an army is dying of thirst in the desert, the voice of God instructs them: "Dig ditches all over this valley. Here's what will happen—you won't hear the wind, you won't see the rain, but this valley is going to fill up with water and your army and your animals will drink their fill. This is easy for God to do". If you can faithfully embody and truly believe in your desired PRL, even when you cannot see the tiniest bit of physical evidence for it, it can and will materialize miraculously.

There is also a broader challenge to address, one that sensitive and empathic souls especially struggle with. Many people resent the fact that certain PRLs exist in the first place. It is natural for a compassionate person to learn that God is infinite creative love and then wonder why God even ALLOWS the possibility of PRLs in which there is disease, poverty, pain, and suffering. Remember, in God's mind, there is no judgment. God must be the ALL; if there were something outside God, that would imply there is more than one God or that God is not infinite. God is all-encompassing and every set of experiences, regardless of the polarity of good-bad, right-wrong, desirable-undesirable, and so forth, is a means through which God experiences his infinitude.

Resenting the possibility of certain undesirable PRLs and trying to "eliminate" them is equivalent to trying to eliminate a piece of God; it simply cannot be done, and the more you resist or attack PRLs you find undesirable, the more they will persist in your physical reality. Your dislike of them will, ironically, draw them into your life. **Thankfully, there is a simple but stunningly effective solution to this: Accept that all PRLs have a place in God, who is ALL THAT IS.** You may not desire them, and you don't have to choose them, but they have a right to exist. You have been given the divine right, as a child of the Creator, to pick whatever you want. Simply choose the PRL you want without fearing, judging, or condemning the PRLs that contain experiences you don't want. Then, only what you desire will become your physical reality.

Factor 4: Extreme Seriousness

Seriousness is a major source of friction that clogs the divine printer. It is difficult to quantify or define precisely what seriousness is, but in general, it is a sense of obsessive "dedication" to attempting to push the new PRL into physical reality rather than simply BEING it and letting it unfold naturally into physical reality with childlike faith, spontaneity, lightness, and cheerfulness. As the master teacher Paramahansa Yogananda noted, the spiritually awakened person "becomes just like a little child, without resentment, without attachment, full of life and joy".

Friction is dense, heavy, attached to outcomes, dependent, and burdensome; faith is light, unconditionally loving, independent, detached, and self-assured no matter what. In the process of Paramorphing to a new PRL, it is common for people to wonder if they are thinking the right thoughts, acting the right way, and taking the right actions in their physical reality. All this leads to overanalytical thinking and worrying, including the concern that doing or not doing some particular action will "ruin" one's desired PRL from materializing.

The other issue is that seriousness creates friction by forgetting the crux of what Paramorphing is truly about. **God limited himself in infinite forms to have fun!** God is infinite light, love, peace, and fun, and becoming obsessively serious about maintaining a certain routine, for example, by writing down or affirming your desires a certain number of times a day, turns what should be a fun and effortless process into one filled with monotony and frustration. There is nothing wrong with maintaining such a routine if it fills you with gladness, joy, and the feeling of embodying your new PRL; however, if it turns into a dreary and tedious chore, there is nothing wrong with scrapping it. YOU are the process, the way, the light, and the life, and you alone give power to your reality.

Reducing seriousness does not mean that you should waver in your conviction of already being in your new PRL. This should be rock-solid. However, you will notice that seriousness is associated with the PRL of NOT YET having what you desire, while fun, lightness, and playful curiosity are born of the state of divine trust and faith, knowing that what you truly feel yourself to be MUST come to pass in your physical reality, no matter what actions you do or don't do. Playfulness and lightness come from realizing that you already have all PRLs within you, no matter what! The legendary spiritual master Krishna was a perfect embodiment of God's light and playful spirit. As a child, he would have fun breaking pots of butter and innocently flirting with the cowgirls of his village, but internally, he always knew his true identity as an omnipotent child of God who was capable of everything and who contained all PRLs inside him. During the Battle of Kurukshetra, Krishna showed the warrior Arjuna his gigantic universal form, or Vishwaroopam. Arjuna realized that Krishna was not actually a small human made of flesh and blood. Krishna was actually the entire cosmos, with an infinite array of PRLs superimposed on top of one another. Krishna's playfulness makes perfect sense. When you are a child of God with infinity at your fingertips, why would you take anything too seriously? Jesus knew and lived the same truth, declaring "my yoke is easy, and my burden is light". Nothing is that serious when you know you can access infinity.

If you consciously examine the world you have created for yourself now, you will notice that many of your most glorious and effortless triumphs came about when you enjoyed the process of going through an experience without worrying about receiving the result in physical reality. A classic example many people on earth can relate to is job interviews. You may have had job interviews that you cared deeply about and studied intensely for. However, your intense desire may have caused you to stumble nervously during the interview. On the flip side, you may have had interviews that you attended with no expectation or burden of performance. Ironically, you enjoyed yourself through the entire interview process, had fun, and were offered the role while beating out other applicants who cared much more about the role.

Faith is playful, and light, and knows that with God, truly ANYTHING and EVERYTHING is possible. By embracing a sense of fun in the process of picking your new PRL, you accept, and even enjoy the current PRL, without painfully tolerating it and desperately hoping for it to disappear.

Rather than worrying about what people will think of you and how circumstances will unfold, simply follow your highest excitement, intuitively doing the things that you are guided to do while personifying the new PRL in your mind. Your conscious mind may not know it, but your divine mind linked to the Eternal Cosmic Library of infinite PRLs, knows exactly how to morph your physical reality into any PRL you can imagine and authentically embody.

By following the impulses that you find fun, joyful, exciting, and intrinsically compelling, you are listening to and acting on the hints that God is providing to reach your new PRL in the most efficient way possible. **Heartfelt excitement, joyful love, and playful curiosity are the strongest markers of God's divine energy.**

Humans on earth are plagued by a chronic sense of unease with being happy, believing that it is somehow immature, childish, or impractical to always be cheerful. Many believe that it is somehow irresponsible, "unrealistic", or even wishful thinking to only do the things your heart truly goads you to do. This is part of the amnesic veil of coming to earth. In reality, the more you heed the inner voice of playfulness, lightness, and spontaneous joy while staying adaptive and flexible, the more quickly you will traverse the path that leads to your new PRL, even though it might not seem logical to your limited conscious mind.

For instance, suppose your desired PRL is to have excellent hearing and overcome a chronic hearing loss condition that plagues you. You claim the new PRL in your imagination and now rejoice, knowing that because you have it in your imagination, it must follow in your physical reality. One day, you wake up and have a strange compelling to go to the park, something which you never generally do. Your conscious mind feels it would be illogical to go to the park now since you have to get ready for your day job, yet a deep impulse inside you urges you to take the morning off and go to the park instead. Curious, you heed your inner intuition and head down to the park and notice a poster on a bulletin board from a local research university testing a novel therapy for treating age-related hearing loss. You call the number on the flyer, and it turns out they have one slot left in the free program. You enroll. If you had followed your logical conscious mind's dictates, you would have gone to your day job and may have never seen the poster that changed your life. You complete the program, and it turns out, your hearing loss is cured fully and permanently. This is just one example, among an infinite number of possibilities, of how heeding your inner voice can effortlessly open doors that your conscious, rational, and linear human mind could never fathom.

As children, you knew that following your heart's excitement and deepest curiosities led to wonderful results and discoveries, yet you stifled this precious gift as you grew up into the fabric of "adulthood" that human society imposes on children, eventually turning them from sparkling conduits of curiosity and divine intuition to broken cogs that languish with their dreams unfulfilled.

You must rekindle this inner spark and fuel it as often as possible, knowing that playfulness is the nature of God, I AM.

When you truly internalize that all things you desire are already yours and that there is a version of you in an adjacent PRL already experiencing life with any desire you might have, why should you be serious? Why would you try so hard when that PRL has already been created and is literally just waiting for you to say YES to come into physical existence? Relax and rejoice! You do not have to struggle and expend effort to be deserving of anything you desire, nor can anything ever be lost. It is all yours and you were born worthy of it.

There are no conditions to be met such as thinking about your desired PRL a certain number of times, writing about it a certain number of times, avoiding negative thoughts, or following whatever else you believe is necessary. You can affirm, imagine, script, and do anything else you want, but do it from the joyful state of knowing it is all already yours, rather than desperately trying to will it into reality with laborious and arduous desperation. If contrary thoughts rise up, simply notice them without resistance or emotional engagement, then decisively shift your attention back to being in your desired PRL. All you want already belongs to you, if you could only have the courage to trust that the higher God-mind in your heart will steer you to it perfectly.

Factor 5: Insufficient Surrender

The experience of being human can be tremendously anxiety-inducing from the standpoint of the conscious mind, for there is seemingly only a tiny slice of reality that is accessible to your conscious mind. It might feel as if you only have a small amount of control over your life experience, while there seem to be an infinite number of other external factors beyond your control. Most humans are so used to the expectation of things turning out poorly for them that at any given juncture, their mind is occupied with a thousand worries about how things could go wrong, how life is fragile, and how the physical body is susceptible to physical, emotional, and mental damage. While people do not necessarily consciously voice these concerns all the time, there is an underlying sense of fear and anxiety about being a limited mortal being that is vulnerable to death, disease, and disappointment.

When a person first learns the truth that he is actually the sole creator of his entire reality and can move to any PRL he desires, there is a tremendous initial burst of joy and enthusiasm. Any PRL can be instantly claimed in one's imaginative sense of I AM. You can mentally embody being in a new PRL immediately. However, the unfolding of this new PRL in the physically dense Earth realm requires the rearrangement of objects and people in time and space. The earth realm affords souls the opportunity to learn patience and trust to a much greater degree than other realms, but many people find themselves frustrated at the speed at which a newly desired PRL turns into physical reality and try to force it to appear more quickly. Or, out of a sense of doubt and fear, they may try to micromanage events, people, and circumstances to attempt to bring about their desired PRL in a way their limited conscious mind can fathom, predict, and control. There is nothing wrong with taking action toward a PRL, of course, but they must flow naturally from the inner state of already BEING in the new PRL and knowing it is already yours.

However, attempting to physically coerce the divine printer only congests it, as shown in the parable of the sun and the wind. Nervousness and anxiety over HOW the new PRL will be brought into physical reality both ruin your inner sense of well-being and prevent the divine printer from working as it should. When your limited human mind decides to take the reins and direct how a new PRL should come into being, the God-mind that has access to the Eternal Cosmic Library of infinite possibilities disengages. That divine mind, your higher God-self, knows the most seamless, efficient, and natural way to bring about your chosen PRL into reality, but when you assert conscious and obsessive control over people, places, and events, you are effectively telling the divine mind "I know how to bring about this new PRL into reality". And the divine printer, which never judges, simply responds "OK, as you wish, you can take over!" and stops using its infinite intelligence to effortlessly morph you into your newly chosen PRL.

Therefore, once you mentally embody your new PRL in imagination, interact with the world in a joyful manner, knowing that you can do no wrong. Know truly and deeply that everything you do or don't do is leading you to the embodiment of the new PRL, and that the divine mind that lies in your heart zone will prompt you to take the right actions at the right time (if any actions are necessary on your part in the first place). You do not have to figure it out. Your job is to select the new PRL and rest knowing it is done. This is why the mystic Paul the Apostle exhorted people to "rejoice always, pray continually, give thanks in all circumstances". This is not merely a trite feel-good platitude but a teaching that contains deep wisdom. By thanking and accepting any circumstance, you are judging it to be a stepping-stone leading to your desired PRL! And, of course, the divine printer of creation will reflect exactly that. If, however, you look at a seemingly undesirable circumstance as proof of not having what you wanted, the divine printer will have no choice but to reflect that instead. In the same way that intense pressure can turn even coal into diamonds, your infinitely powerful I AM awareness can convert even seemingly hopeless circumstances into miraculous successes. It might seem simplistic or even childish to simply blindly assume that everything is going well and that everything is working out perfectly. Yet, this is the wisest way to live. **When you truly believe that everything around you is unfolding perfectly, you are making the entire universe work on your behalf to materialize your desires.** Everything will conspire in your favor. It must!

At best, the smartest human mind can arrange a few people, circumstances, and events toward a certain outcome. The higher intelligence of the divine mind can move a billion people in a precisely orchestrated sequence to bring about the realization of your desired PRL in the most effortless and efficient way possible. It is downright foolish to try and understand the power of your higher, N-dimensional God-self with your limited 3-dimensional human mind.

To NOT faithfully surrender to the infinitely intelligent higher power would be the height of foolishness, yet that is how almost all humans on earth attempt to change their reality. They overthink and overvalue the physical actions they take in influencing people and events, without realizing that the higher power of God within them could instantly accomplish feats that the smartest human could not achieve with lifetimes worth of effort. When Jesus taught "with men this is impossible, but with God all things are possible", he wasn't merely offering a sweet-sounding statement of hope. He was expressing the absolute truth.

Ironically, then, the best way to maintain control and certainty over knowing you will have your desired physical reality is to let go! It is a paradox, but in Paramorphing, paradoxes are a sign that you have discovered a divine truth.

Once you let go of trying to frantically micromanage events in time and space, the higher divine mind, linked to your heart zone, will move you from your current PRL to your new PRL by morphing you through countless INTERMEDIARY PRLs. We call this the **Paramorphing Chain.** Once you provide the divine printer a new state or identity, and decide with conviction to embody that PRL, it will sketch the most efficient path to materialize that new PRL in a way that will not overwhelm your conscious mind on earth. Your conscious mind thrives on a sense of stability. For the average person, life would become chaotic and frighteningly unpredictable if everything they thought of instantly became a physical reality. To prevent the conscious mind from being overwhelmed, the divine mind of God morphs you into your newly embodied PRL by shifting you gradually and subtly through a chain of thousands of intermediary PRLs that the conscious mind could never fathom. The gradient colors used in the cover of this book represent how smoothly and subtly this morphing process works.

What might this Paramorphing Chain look like? The divine mind can accomplish an infinite number of changes in a single instant, but here is a small example of what it could be like. Suppose you are a real estate developer, and you would like to clear trees from a plot of land before you build a housing development on it. However, you are short on funds and cannot afford a landscaping company to uproot the trees. You use your conscious logical mind to contact as many landscaping companies as possible and even try the forceful approach of offering your employees extra cash if they help uproot the trees on the weekend, but none of them really want to. In fact, some are offended that you have even asked.

Exhausted, you quit trying to change circumstances with force, and simply visualize that you have already moved to your desired PRL in which the land is clean and smooth. You don't worry about how the trees were removed or how you obtained the funds to do so. You simply focus on your desired PRL, imagining your plot of land to be smooth and treeless NOW and feel a sense of relief and deep gladness that you are already in your new PRL. Now, unbeknownst to you, the divine mind has already sketched the Paramorphing Chain to materialize your desired PRL. First, it prompts a furniture maker in a foreign city to search for a specific type of wood to make custom cabinets requested by a customer. Second, it guides that furniture marker to learn about your plot of land, which happens to have the type of wood he requires. Third, it prompts the furniture maker to reach out to you and offer to pay for the wood on your plot of land. Fourth, the divine mind intuitively nudges you to offer something that is a perfect win-win solution: You tell the furniture maker he can have the wood for a steep discount if he pays for the cost of uprooting the trees and cleaning up the plot. In the end, you didn't just receive your desired PRL;

you received something even better. Rather than paying someone to uproot the trees, you got someone to pay you to uproot the trees!

This is just one small example of how the divine mind's infinite intelligence can bring about gloriously efficient outcomes that your limited conscious mind could never know how to engineer and synchronize into physical reality.

Now, you may wonder if it is possible to morph to PRLs within designated time and space boundaries, such as "by tomorrow afternoon, I will have received $1 million". Can you? Of course. There is a PRL for every imaginative scenario you can picture. However, the more specific the conditions and parameters you place, the **cleaner** and **purer** your faith needs to be. Only an absolute master or wizard who internalizes Paramorphing to the highest degree would have the necessary faith to pull this off, for when you try to control the time and space regarding a new PRL, you will ONLY succeed if you have perfect faith and absolutely no friction in the form of doubts and fears. The slightest bit of friction, in this case, will clog the divine printer. If you have the perfect faith of a spiritual master such as Jesus, you most certainly can decree the exact parameters of time and space, including the specific way a particular PRL should unfold in the Paramorphing Chain, and you can materialize it. You can order mountains to be cast into the sea in the blink of an eye, and they will. If you, however, do not have such perfect faith, simply trust that the higher mind knows how to morph time and space to bring about your desired PRL in the most efficient and natural way possible. Then, let go of your worries regarding how and when. The irony is when you stop trying to "fast-track" your desired PRLs and simply surrender to the Paramorphing Chain dictated by the divine mind, circumstances morph more fluidly and rapidly toward your desired end.

Factor 6: Lack of True Desire

One of the most underrated sources of friction for people on earth is pursuing goals, experiences, and PRLs that they truly do not desire, but rather have been forced upon them by societal, cultural, and familial expectations. Your heart's Harmonic Signature is infinitely unique and no one but you can truly know the specific PRL that fills you with gladness and fulfillment. Society cannot possibly understand this and will try to shove you into a one-size-fits-all energetic signature that will slowly smother your inner fire and zest for life.

Societal, cultural, and familial norms vary based on time periods, trends, and cultural expectations, but the one thing they have in common is that they force a cookie-cutter PRL on individuals, without regard for what truly makes a person's heart sing. Even souls that start off fiery, rebellious, and independent as children often become muted, despondent, and timid by adulthood, as they are brainwashed into giving up their deepest dreams and desires.

You know what makes your heart sing. You know, deep down, the precise set of experiences that intrinsically fill you with joy. You know, deep down, the exact type of life partner and friends that would be perfect for you. And you know, without a shadow of a doubt, how much money you truly desire, the perfect career that fills you with excitement when you wake up each day in the morning, and the objects and possessions that you truly wish to have and enjoy, whether it be a brick-faced 4-bedroom home in a suburb, a steel espresso machine, or a nautical-blue SUV. In other words, you know, at the very core of your being, the precise set of PRLs that make your soul light up and sparkle with that intangible sense of deep happiness, inner warmth, fulfillment, and gratitude. No one has to tell you these things. You simply know what they are, though you may repress your deepest longings because your society and culture might suggest otherwise. You might be told your desires are impractical, delusional, or even that you are not worthy of them.

At the very least, even if you don't know the precise PRLs that will make your heart sing, you know what it feels like when all is right in the world. Each person can recollect times in their lives during which they finally achieved, accomplished, or received something they had deeply desired for a significant period of time. When you finally receive the object or experience, whether it is a specific possession such as a beautiful house or an experience such as a passionate kiss from a person you fancied for years, you descend into an indescribably pure sense of glad contentment, not caring if the world were to end at that moment, because you are happy, full, and complete. Fulfillment is your truest identity.

This all-enveloping fullness and deeply peaceful joy is the pure state of I AM. The moment you receive a burning desire, you are filled with joy, contentment, and peace. In other words, you are filled with the holy spirit, God, who is never in a state of lack but contains all PRLs in his divine and infinite Eternal Cosmic Library.

How can you tell if something is a truly burning desire, something which you intrinsically desire? It is simple. Upon imagining that you are in the PRL of already having received it, see how you feel. If a feeling of spontaneous peace, gladness, fullness, and gratitude flood your being, and if your logical conscious mind goes blank, stops thinking, and dips into the warm glow of your heart zone, you can be assured that this is a true heart's desire.

Why does it matter if a wish is a burning heart's desire or merely something that you may have lukewarm feelings toward because it was imposed upon you by social expectations? For the simple reason that a true heart's desire is ALREADY GUARANTEED to be yours, for it will contain zero friction. If you spontaneously feel a deep sense of childlike gratefulness or even genuine relief about receiving a desire, it is MEANT FOR YOU, and not a single force in the universe can stop you from Paramorphing to the PRL where you experience it in physical reality. No barriers can stop you when your heart truly wishes for something. Having a deep desire means that there is a parallel version of you in a very close-by PRL already experiencing the desire in physical reality! So let go, relax, and rejoice. To deeply desire a PRL means it is already yours and quite literally God's wish for you to experience that.

Remember, God seeks to experientially know himself through you. Your role as a child of God is priceless. You are the vehicle, the channel, through which God can experience different aspects of himself. You have access to all PRLs, but in any given lifetime, you can only experience a small fraction of the eternity that you are. Deep desire is the language God uses to inform you which PRLs you will find most fulfilling in your current lifetime. **Your deepest heart's desires are not childish delusions but GOD HIMSELF telling you what he would like to experience through your physical vehicle.** When God wants something, do you think he can be denied? Can he fail? Obviously not. Listening to your deepest desires is how you co-create with God.

A heart's desire is an absolute conviction to have a particular PRL, no matter what. The underlying energetic frequency of a heart's desire is "this is mine", an absolute sense of certainty in moving into the state of BEING that new PRL, irrespective of the friction created by doubt or fear. The heart's power of infinite love can and will obliterate any amount of doubt, fear, or uncertainty.

When the heart zone is activated, the entire power of the universe conspires in your favor. Heaven and earth start moving in order to materialize your desired PRL. Words cannot describe the depth and magnitude of this divine power. It brings one to tears.

You can, of course, also Paramorph to PRLs that you do not have a burning desire for. There might be more friction, and the divine printer might experience more congestion in the process of transmuting your imagined PRL to physical reality, but it is still possible. That being said, if you do choose a PRL that is not a true heart's desire, you will have to live with the disappointment of settling for less than what you truly wanted. If you had submitted to your heart's desire, no matter what, the entire cosmos would have conspired to make your PRL a physical reality. For instance, suppose you are a man from a religiously conservative family who truly loves a particular woman of a different religion and wishes to marry her, but doesn't know how your family would tolerate this. Suppose your burning desire is to marry the woman who makes your heart sing and to also have her lovingly accepted as a daughter-in-law by your parents. This PRL will most certainly become your physical reality, if only you could have the courage to claim it. Do not worry about the conscious logical mind which wonders, for instance, how a religiously conservative family could ever accept a girl from a different religion as one of their own. The I AM in your heart zone contains ALL THINGS, including a PRL in which your wish already exists as a solid, tangible physical reality. The price you pay to possess and experience this reality is your unwavering faith in that PRL and the power of your inner I AM to breathe life into it.

We will end with one small example that shows how the power of a heart's desire leads to herculean feats beyond rational explanation. There are countless examples, if you wish to search for them, of small women and unathletic men, with no training, lifting cars in order to save their loved ones after crashes. Even trained strength athletes would find it tremendously difficult to lift a multi-ton vehicle, yet there are 120-lb mothers who have done this in order to save their children trapped in vehicles.

When a mother sees her child trapped in a vehicle that could end his life, the entire world goes blank for her. Doubt, frustration, fears, and worries go into the garbage bin and are replaced by a single, steely conviction that "I will save my beloved child, no matter what". Scientists on earth call this phenomenon "hysterical strength", displays of "unusual" capabilities far beyond what is "normal" for humans. However, the capabilities are neither unusual nor abnormal. When a person is absolutely locked into a heart's desired PRL (such as the PRL in which a beloved family member is safe and sound), this perfect faith in the desired reality channels the limitless energy of Source to flow through her so she can accomplish whatever is necessary to materialize the desired PRL. When the infinite power of God is channeled, all things are possible. Not many, not most, but ALL things.

Factor 7: Habituation to the Past

The final, and perhaps most underrated, source of friction is habituation to past PRLs. It seems ludicrous to think that one could not only tolerate but also enjoy and quietly crave PRLs of lack, limitation, pain, and suffering, but it is quite common on earth.

Despair, whining, complaining, and suffering all carry a secret perverse pleasure. There is a comfortable joy in resigning yourself to hopelessness, procuring sympathy from others, and feeling as if the world is "out to get me". When one deeply believes in this paradigm, the mind unconsciously grows attached to the pain and suffering, for it provides a sense of identity as a "sufferer" or one who is "battling hardships" and therefore deserves sympathy.

The state of being in a PRL of lack, limitation, despair, and sadness is addictive. At the very least, whether a person knows it or not, there is a subtle energetic signature associated with each PRL. From God's standpoint, of course, no PRL is objectively good or bad, desirable or undesirable; they all simply exist because God IS. For that reason, the divine printer never judges if someone chooses to dwell in any PRL. PRLs crystallize into physical reality when a person authentically and feelingly embodies them by linking them to their innate divine sense of I AM, which is the spark of God in all souls. When a person has remained in a particular PRL for a period of time, such as I AM A CHRONIC SUFFERER or LIFE IS A STRUGGLE, the PRL gains a life of its own, so to speak, and the person begins to deeply radiate the PRL's energetic signature.

The most surprising part is that because any PRL has the potential to become authentically embodied, a person who has dwelled in a PRL of complaining about financial hardship, for instance, may actually feel GREATER discomfort when he first starts assuming a newly desired PRL of financial abundance. On paper, this makes no sense. Energetically, however, it is perfectly understandable. The old PRL and its associated tendencies, which have been reinforced into the person's physical reality for months, years, and perhaps even decades, have built an energetic scaffolding that the person takes to be "normal" and "comfortable". Any energetic change, such as a shift to a new PRL and energetic identity. is perceived as a threat by the current PRL identity, no matter how materially beneficial it might be.

In other words, because God never judges any PRL and views all of them with an equal gaze, it is perfectly common to find yourself clinging to seemingly undesirable PRLs, and feeling a great pull from your former PRL identity as you switch to your newly desired PRL. Must this always be the case? Of course not. If you have decided, with absolute conviction, that you are your new PRL and nothing else can deter you, the divine printer will rapidly and faithfully morph you into the new PRL. However, it is possible for you to be challenged by seemingly undesirable or even contrary circumstances as you move into your new PRL. Certain schools of teaching refer to these as "tests from the universe", but there is no universe testing you. The simple truth is that your own prior dwelling in certain PRLs has created a certain energetic state of familiarity, and you are merely redefining yourself with your new PRL identity. If there is anyone or anything testing you, it is only you. Do you truly possess the conviction to move into your new PRL, no matter what circumstances show or what you may have been in the past? Only you can answer this question, and you answer it through the way you choose to respond to your circumstances.

Let us illustrate this with an example. Suppose you are a female who lives close to your in-laws, and you find your mother-in-law incredibly judgmental, ungrateful, and cantankerous. After learning about Paramorphing, you realize that you have created your entire reality and that you can immediately morph into an already existing PRL in which your mother-in-law loves, cherishes, and respects you. With great enthusiasm, you go to bed at night declaring I AM IN MY NEW PRL, fall asleep with a smile on your face, and the next morning, your mother-in-law visits you with a thoughtful present. How wonderful! You feel Paramorphing is, indeed, real. This pleasant mood continues for a few days.

The following week, your mother-in-law visits you, but the pleasantries have been replaced by carping, complaining, and criticism. You feel deeply hurt and begin to wonder whether Paramorphing is actually real or simply some new-age nonsense that is too good to be true. At this CRUCIAL juncture, you have two options. Option one would be to succumb to your negative emotions, assume that Paramorphing is nonsense, and go back to your usual perception of your mother-in-law as a cranky and vile woman. Somehow, though you want her to treat you better, you feel oddly comfortable in defining her this way and enduring her poor treatment. Option two is to recognize you are being tested, not by any external force, but by yourself! The old PRL in which you had a poor relationship with your mother-in-law doesn't want to die, for it has built up an energetic signature and life of its own. You realize that you must persist in your new PRL of imagining a harmonious relationship between you and your mother-in-law, no matter what, and firmly move to the inner conviction that I AM IN MY NEW PRL, no matter what physical circumstances show. You move to the inner certainty that you are the center of your reality and that the divine printer of physical reality has NO CHOICE but to eventually reflect your inner state of BEING.

If you follow Option 1, you will find yourself sliding back into the old, current, familiar PRL. If you follow Option 2, you will find yourself eventually breaking through, and the divine printer will have no choice but to recognize that you are authentically embodying a new PRL and new energetic state of being, and print that out into physical reality.

Nothing, truly, can take the place of persistent conviction. God does not beg, plead, whine, or doubt. God declares I AM and simply claims a new PRL with kingly authority and poise, knowing that all PRLs are subordinate to him, for he is the Creator and Source of ALL THAT IS. You are made in God's image.

Will you doubtfully fiddle with your reality with your limited human mind, or will you firmly Paramorph to a new PRL by harnessing your inner Godhood? Only you can decide this.

Now, of course, it is important to not be too hard on yourself if you catch yourself slipping from the state of having your new PRL. All you have to do is honestly examine yourself, and move back into the state of having your new PRL whenever you catch yourself lapsing back into old energetic patterns associated with the PRL you have chosen to exist. Remember, nothing is ever lost. You create your ENTIRE PHYSICAL REALITY, past, present, and future from the PRL you are embodying HERE AND NOW. You can change everything, including the past, NOW. It might seem ludicrous to the human mind, which conceives reality in a linear way, but the truth is that by embodying a new identity NOW, you choose a new past, present, and future. I AM, the essence of God, precedes and transcends time and space. When you authentically Paramorph into a new identity and PRL, you quite literally bend and warp the 3D fabric of time and space. You aren't changing or destroying your old PRL, for all PRLs exist forever in the Eternal Cosmic Library. Rather, you are simply moving to a new PRL which comes equipped with a new past and future. The beauty of Paramorphing is that you do not have to figure out the complicated details of your new identity. Your higher God-self takes care of this with its infinite power. All you have to do, with your conscious mind, is to definitively choose and embody the state of already being in your new PRL.

Creation requires cremation. You cannot straddle two PRLs, with one foot in each. You can EITHER be in the old PRL OR in the new one. Cremate the old PRL, your old identity, and everything associated with it, by removing all your attention from it. Do not fight it, for fighting a PRL means you dwell on it, and dwelling on it sustains it in your physical reality. Simply turn your attention away from the old PRL and place it squarely on your new PRL. Your attention is the fertilizer that causes any PRL to blossom into physical reality. To kill an old PRL, you simply need to take your attention away from it, and it will shrivel and die off. Let unwanted PRLs dissolve without forcibly trying to push them out.

In reality, though, you are not dissolving some external PRL "out there". You are dying to your old self-definition, and moving to a new self-definition of who you are, a new concept of yourself. You move to a new I AM identity.

We have now covered the 7 sources of friction that can congest the divine printer of physical reality. Staying aware of them will enable you to Paramorph more quickly, seamlessly, and confidently to your new desired PRL.

* * * * * * * * * *

Chapter 6: The Practical Application of Paramorphing

It is natural to want to use Paramorphing to change physical reality. That is the entire point, in some sense, of being born as humans. Souls descend to earth and agree to undergo the amnesic veil so they can richly experience physical life as human beings, which affords a certain "density" of experience that the less dense astral realms cannot provide. It is completely natural, therefore, to want to change your PRL and experience your heart's desires.

We have made it clear that all PRLs exist as eternal templates in the Eternal Cosmic Library, the mind of God, and that any physical reality is merely a printout of one of those infinite PRLs. We have also made it clear that the physical world is merely a shadow and not the causal factor of reality. The true cause of a person's life experience is the PRL he truly feels and embodies mentally; in other words, he is conscious of BEING in his imagination.

If we understand this deeply, we should realize that the true reality is our imagination. We should be completely and utterly satisfied upon accepting a PRL in imagination alone, rather than waiting for it to materialize in physical reality. If you are "waiting for a new PRL", the divine printer will simply print out a physical reality in which you are perpetually waiting for the new reality instead of actually receiving it. Hence, the core of Paramorphing is to truly feel and know that what you desire has already been given to you and to let your emotions, actions, and thoughts naturally flow from occupying the new PRL.

Though imagination is the cause of reality, humans naturally desire physical experiences. People choose to be born on Earth to experience sensations and pleasures in physical reality, whether it be performing music in front of thousands of people, feeling the lips of a romantic partner on one's body, or experiencing the thrill of flying in a luxurious private jet.

For certain burning desires, a person may find it nearly impossible to merely remain patient until the PRL appears in physical reality. He might find it unsatisfactory to simply accept that his new PRL is already his and will unfold in physical reality now that he has accepted his desire. If he impatiently persists in craving and longing for the physical appearance of his desired PRL, he will generate tremendous friction that delays his new PRL from materializing. In truth, you can morph into ANY reality simply by maintaining childlike faith and conviction that you already have it. However, due to human limitations and friction, we will discuss a practical process for realistically embodying the state of having your chosen PRL here and now.

The first step is to develop the self-control to completely untether oneself from the physical world and start solely defining oneself in imagination alone. Fully accept that your inner conception of yourself is who you TRULY are and the creative cause of your external reality. This, for example, is why wealthy people who lose tremendous amounts of money soon find themselves to be wealthy once more, while poor individuals who come into financial windfalls like lottery wins soon find themselves back in a state of poverty if their inner self-image (or self-imagination!) has not changed.

In imagination, the friction-inducing states of craving and desperation are impossible, as you can instantly have whatever your heart desires. The focused exercise of imagination is perhaps the most pleasurable and rewarding activity a person can engage in, but years of merely consuming content on earth have nearly completely atrophied the average person's ability to imagine richly and vividly. Due to the rise of quick-consumption video formats and platforms that destroy attention spans, the average person has developed a tremendous ability to superficially consume large amounts of short-span content but their ability to expansively imagine and create sensorily rich visualization scenes has been utterly destroyed.

The good news, however, is that imagination is a muscle, and even atrophied muscles can regain their former strength and flexibility when they are regularly exercised. Some people are naturally gifted with a rich imaginative faculty, but everyone can make substantial gains regardless of their starting point.

In Paramorphing, there are two primary ways to leverage imagination to embody your desired PRL. The first is the Inside-Out method, the imaginative process of going to your I AM center and robustly experiencing your desired PRL with great sensory realism. The second is the Outside-In method, the process of "overlaying" your desired PRL on your waking reality until your desired PRL feels natural to you as an integrated part of your daily life. By imagining yourself already experiencing your desired PRL, you authentically define your identity as the person who is already in your new desired PRL, which rapidly reduces friction and allows your chosen PRL to materialize in physical reality.

The Inside-Out Method

Embodying Desired PRLs

The Inside-Out Method requires you to first access the state of pure I AM that lies within you. Your I AM is the only absolute reality, the pure consciousness that contains all PRL templates and can morph you into any of them. Your I AM is your magic carpet, your savior, that can free you from any PRL and move you to another one. For those who are familiar with driving stick-shift automobiles, your I AM can be compared to the clutch pedal on a car that disengages your current gear (your old/existing PRL) and allows you to shift into any other gear (your new/desired PRL).

How do you access this pure I AM? Well, in truth, it is not

"difficult" to realize your inner God-being because it is who you fundamentally are. No matter what PRL you might be playing in your physical reality right now, all the forms, people, events, and objects are really just dream illusions while there is only ONE objective reality that gives rise to all of them: Pure consciousness, the divine I AM, that is God. The only issue is that for most people, while they are awake, their minds create so much noise in the form of thoughts, that this underlying God-consciousness is obscured (though, of course, never destroyed, because it is the only eternal reality).

We could take an entire book to discuss how to reach the state of I AM. In fact, that is the only topic of any true spiritual teaching, whether one looks at the works of Christian mysticism, Vedanta, Sufism, or other traditions. The central directive of any great spiritual work is providing guideposts, signs, and clues to help readers realize who they truly are: Pure, eternal, and divine consciousness enjoying temporary physical experiences as distinct and separate forms. When the conscious human mind, energetically centered in the head zone, becomes less active and more still, it automatically starts dipping toward the heart zone, where one can access the I AM or divine infinite mind of God that contains all PRLs. It is pure, formless awareness.

In order to change your reality, your mind's attention must be in between the heart and the head zones. The head zone is your regular waking consciousness (what neuroscience calls the beta brainwave state) in which you are experiencing a particular PRL, but do not have the capacity to change it. The heart zone is where your conscious mind dissolves into the mind of God and replenishes itself during deep sleep. In deep sleep, you enter the delta brainwave state. Here, you have access to ALL PRLs in God's Eternal Cosmic Library but do not have the attentive capacity to choose a new PRL because your conscious mind is absent. Upon waking, in a split second, your conscious mind asserts itself as a separate entity, picks a PRL from the heart zone, and rushes to your head zone, displaying this PRL as your perceived physical reality. Since most people never truly make changes at the heart zone level, the PRL that their mind broadcasts each day looks almost exactly the same.

The key to Paramorphing is to access the twilight states that exist between the beta-brainwave state of waking consciousness and the delta-brainwave state of deep sleep. Science calls these states "alpha" and "theta", but there are actually an infinite number of "semi-conscious" intermediary states between waking consciousness and sleeping unconsciousness. In this precious intermediary zone of semi-consciousness, one has access to both the head and the heart zones, retaining the capacity to direct attention toward a desired PRL (the power of the head zone) while also being linked to the infinite Eternal Cosmic Library which can access ALL PRLs (the power of the heart zone). **In this intermediary twilight state, in which head and heart are yoked together, one gains the power to morph into ANY DESIRED PRL.**

One way to slow down the conscious mind is to perform the exercise of self-inquiry as described previously, recognizing experientially that you are the consciousness that remains unchanged even as your body, mind, emotions, thoughts, and feelings change. By enquiring who you are, you will gradually arrive at the deepest and truest layer of your being, the formless and infinitely high-frequency I AM that connects you to all that is. As your spiritual journey continues, you will find that you do not need to set aside designated meditation times to access this formless layer, nor will you need to discipline the mind as much. You will naturally and spontaneously start "falling into" the state of pure consciousness, for it is eternally new, enjoyable, and peaceful. This cannot truly be explained in words. It must be experienced.

A second way is to chant or meditate deeply on passages and mantras written by spiritually awakened men and women, for such writings are charged with the source energy of the divine infinite mind. Certain works such as the Biblical Psalms and the Gayatri Mantra, for instance, automatically slow down the conscious mind upon recitation, whether one understands their meaning or not. Passages written by mystics who have personally experienced the love, power, and peace of God are impregnated with the energy of the divine mind, even after thousands of years. Some examples include the works of Rumi, chapters from Krishna's Bhagavad Gita, verses from the books of Matthew and John in the Bible, Jesus's Sermon on the Mount, the Upanishads, the Prayer of Saint Francis, and the Ashtavakra Gita. However, note that these are merely examples, and in fact, you may find other material, such as a loving letter from a family member or an evocative movie scene, that helps you enter the same inner state of pure being, characterized by an alert peace, deep love, and contentment. The nature of your inner I AM cannot fully be captured in words or descriptions though; it is one with God, and the only thing that can be said is that GOD IS.

A third way to jump-start this inward process is to simply wait until your conscious mind gets tired. In other words, right before you are about to fall asleep, you will notice that you settle into a drowsy state in which you are completely relaxed and free of worrisome thoughts. In this "twilight state", you still remain alert enough to maintain control over your thinking, without falling into a dream or deep sleep state. The advantage and beauty of this approach are that intense self-inquiry, meditation, chanting, and other processes are not necessary; one merely takes advantage of natural biological rhythms that nature provides twice a day (or more frequently if one takes afternoon naps for instance). The body tends to naturally move toward this semi-conscious state after heavy physical exertion, or after eating a meal; afternoon naps after lunch are a great time to enter the twilight state. You can further enhance this process by employing sounds such as binaural beats with headphones, white noise, natural water sounds, relaxing soundscapes, and pan flute music, all of which quieten the conscious mind.

A fourth way to quickly access the deeper dimension of I AM and maintain a twilight state is to visit a place that is charged with the energy of Source. It cannot be described; it can only be felt and grasped with one's inner being. Quiet forests and beaches, for example, possess an uncanny ability to still the loud conscious mind and enable one to access the twilight state of peaceful semi-consciousness. Properly consecrated religious sites of worship, such as temples and churches, often possess a similarly high energetic frequency that quietens the conscious mind because, at these locations, people chant and think about divinely charged names such as Krishna, Jesus, Buddha, Ram, Jehovah, Sai, Aum, Amen, Amin, as well as divine concepts such as peace, love, joy, power, gratitude, and eternal life.

Perhaps the most unique way to directly experience the infinite power of your inner I AM is to go to a tomb or "samadhi" that houses the mortal remains of saints, mystics, and wizards who realized their Oneness with God. The energetic power and mind-stilling peace of such a Self-Realized being radiates from their bones for hundreds, if not thousands, of years after their mortal body passes, which is one reason why saints are buried rather than cremated. As an example, one feels this tremendous and deep sense of peace radiating from the tomb of Saint Francis of Assisi, who awoke to the truth of his inner divinity and became one with Christ during his lifetime. The same is true of places where great spiritual masters dwelled, such as the city of Dwaraka in India, where the great spiritual icon Krishna lived and imparted his wisdom. Remember, you are no less than any such master! You too, are a spiritual master, and equally divine as a child of the supreme Creator who lies at the very center of your being. When you go to such a place, you are not soliciting some external power. Rather, you are rediscovering the very core of your OWN being and returning back home to your divine Father.

Once you have tapped into the formless, peacefully still, and divine core of your being, I AM, you are ready to start applying the Inside-Out Method. Remember, it is not the technique itself that morphs you into a new PRL. It is the fact that the technique allows you to realistically and naturally EMBODY your new desired PRL, thereby bringing it from the infinite Eternal Cosmic Library of God's divine mind into your selected PRL experience, HERE AND NOW. You are moving from the infinite state of I AM, which has access to all possibilities, to defining yourself as one specific PRL in imagination. You are not begging, craving, or trying. You are simply deciding on a new PRL and moving there.

Close your eyes and make yourself comfortable. You can sit on the floor in a posture that is comfortable to you, such as the lotus position. You could alternatively lay on your bed or recline on a sofa with a leg rest. The specific position does not matter. What matters is that you put yourself in an absolutely comfortable, relaxed, and loose position in a quiet setting, allowing you to exercise your imaginative faculties without the external world disrupting your inner peace.

Once you are comfortable, shut your eyes and relax your hands and legs. It is time to now embody and enter your new PRL. Remember, it is not something to get in the "future". Every PRL exists NOW and right HERE, so there is a version of you already experiencing your desired reality. You are now merely crystallizing it into physical reality with your focus. You aren't creating anything: It has already been made and exists in God's Eternal Cosmic Library.

Immerse yourself in the new PRL by dwelling in it with your inner imaginative sense. Your external sense organs, such as your nose, ears, and eyes, are merely dead conduits that work because your INNER ENERGETIC SENSES flow through them. Do you want proof? It is simple. Right now, think of the smell of apple pie. Hold out your hand and grasp a tennis ball. Hear the sound of a lawnmower. You don't need the presence of apple pie to smell the delicious, subtly rich, and floral aroma of the dish. You don't need a physical tennis ball to feel its light, fuzzy, and slightly itchy exterior in your palm. And you don't need to turn on a lawnmower to hear the guttural roar of its engine. Your INNER ENERGETIC SENSES reproduce all these sensations with stunning fidelity.

Every PRL has trademark "highlight reels", specific sequences of actions and experiences that unmistakably characterize it, and DISTINGUISH IT from your existing PRL. For example, suppose you have endured chronic arthritis for years in your current PRL, and have firmly decided to Paramorph to the PRL in which you are healthy. What makes your heart sing about the new PRL? Remember, the heart zone contains the key to crystallizing any PRL into physical reality, so investigating what it truly loves will bring miracles into your life. When you examine what makes you thrilled about the new PRL, you might find intrinsic, heartfelt joy and gladness about the prospect of finally being able to go on hikes (something you loved when you were younger but had to give up due to arthritis), play baseball with your grandchildren, and dance with your husband (something you cherish dearly).

Now that you know exactly what you love about your new PRL, you will construct a small mental video of a Recurring Highlight Sequence (RHS) in which you combine these wonderful new capabilities into a small, single, 3-5 second mental video which can be looped over and over. The RHS is one of the most powerful Paramorphing techniques, for the repetition involved in the method firmly influences the heart zone to pick and rapidly start crystallizing your new PRL. Repetition also enables you to start feeling a particular scene as a natural, real, and authentic experience rather than a hazy dream. For instance, you might design a scene in which you are on a mountain cabin in your favorite hiking destination, which implies that you, of course, hiked there. Your family is around you and you can hear them. You are dancing with your husband when your grandson comes in and adorably throws a baseball at your thigh, so you laugh, stop your dancing, pick up the baseball, throw it back to him, kiss him on the cheeks, then go back to dancing with your husband. Because the start and end scenes of this sequence are the same (dancing with your husband), you can keep looping this RHS in your inner imaginative faculties as many times as you want.

There is, however, a catch. You are the center of reality, a child of God, so physical reality can only follow and reflect what you claim and appropriate for yourself. That means you will have to not only "play" the RHS in your head as an observer, but as a PARTICIPANT. You will have to use your inner imaginative sense to enter the RHS and experience it in the same way that an actor would play a character in a film. Expert actors do not think about the characters they play. They BECOME the character they play and EMBODY that character fully. You must do the same.

You are literally wearing a skinsuit and entering your new PRL. It is NOT a mere delusion or fantasy. Remember, if you can imagine something, it ALREADY EXISTS AS A CONCRETE PHYSICAL REALITY within the infinite I AM, the divine mind of God, so enjoy and embody it fully. When you enter the mountain cabin, hear the sound of the floor creaking. Smell the polish of the wood and the crisp natural air. Feel the lightness in your healthy legs as you run into the cabin. When you dance with your husband, feel your hand wrapped inside his. Your physical body can remain still because you are relaxed, but your INNER ENERGETIC SENSES, which are the real you, should be active. Your inner imaginative hand can caress your husband's neck, feeling the back collar of his sweater. You smell the lingering fragrance of his cologne. You then feel the soft thud of a kid's baseball against the back of your legs, turn around, and see your grandson. You see his tousled hair and cute smile, and give him a kiss, feeling your lips press against his soft, blushing cheek as he giggles. You then turn back and resume dancing with your husband, feeling his smooth cashmere sweater and his quiet breath against your temples as you dance with him, as a creek gurgles in the background mixed with the chirps of birds.

In other words, you must experience your PRL in the FIRST-PERSON perspective by entering it as someone having the experience HERE AND NOW, rather than viewing it from the THIRD-PERSON perspective (as you would if you were watching a film of someone). If you start viewing the RHS from the THIRD-PERSON perspective (of being an observer rather than the participant), gently catch yourself and shift back into a FIRST-PERSON perspective. It is easy to tell if you have lapsed into a third-person perspective. For example, in your imagination, if you see the back of your body or your own face, this is obviously a third-person perspective! Think about your waking reality right now. Do you see your own face? You don't, except when you're staring at a mirror, taking a selfie, or viewing photographs of yourself. In your normal waking consciousness, you don't see your own face or the back of your body.

Your normal waking consciousness is a FIRST-PERSON perspective of your current PRL. That's why it's the reality you're experiencing now! If you wish to change your reality to a new PRL, your RHS should be a FIRST-PERSON perspective of that newly desired PRL, and it will begin to materialize.

Why is it important to loop your RHS? First, the heart zone is influenced by conviction, repetition, and persistence. Second, it is fairly challenging for most individuals to realistically capture the depth of authenticity associated with a new PRL after immersing themselves in it just once. What is naturalness? It is difficult to describe the concept in words, but the easiest way to understand it is to think about your current waking reality and the PRL you now experience. Think about how comfortable you are with the objects you own, the house you live in, and the car you drive. You almost take them for granted, not in an arrogant or condescending way, but in the matter-of-fact manner of knowing that these things are yours and that you deserve them. You also have a deep and rich knowledge of the sensory details of your current possessions; for example, you know how your car looks, how the interior smells, how the steering wheel feels in your hands, how the seat motors sound when you adjust them, and so forth. You perceive the people close to you with the same, confident sense of knowing. You have an unmistakable feeling of ease and comfort with them and a rich, multi-layered understanding of who they are and how they behave. Your knowing, in short, cannot be faked.

Authenticity is the key to crystallizing any PRL because God is absolute honesty. Just think about the veil of amnesia you threw over yourself when coming to Earth. You decided to totally forget about the fact that you are God in order to realistically and authentically experience what it would feel like to be a human being. This is how committed you are, as a divine child of God, to experiencing PRLs richly and realistically! Now, to Paramorph to new PRLs, the same dedication is required. You must embody your new PRL, here and now, fully and genuinely.

By looping your RHS, you build authenticity in truly defining yourself as the new PRL. In the case of our example here, suppose you play the RHS of dancing with your husband in a mountain cabin you've hiked to, while your grandson throws a baseball at you. The first time you run this RHS in your imagination, you might merely have a fuzzy outline of the RHS. Colors may barely be visible, and the entire sequence might seem grainy and distorted like an old videotape. That's ok. Be gentle with yourself, and simply make the loop better each time by enriching the sensory detail. For instance, the second time you play the loop, focus on colors, appreciating your husband's richly colored scarlet cashmere sweater, the emerald greenery of the trees outside, and the golden-brown oak floor planks of the cabin. The third time, retain all of these color cues, but add the sound of your grandson's cute giggle, the gurgling creek outside, and your husband's soft breath. The fourth time, retain both color and sound cues and add the olfactory sensations of the earthy wood smell in the cabin and your husband's masculine tobacco-scented cologne. The fifth time, retain all of your rich visual, auditory, and olfactory cues while adding the FEELING of being in the new PRL.

How does it feel? Only you can answer this question! Remember, the heart zone's energy is a pure, non-judgmental, loving conviction that grants whatever PRL a person asks for, and its sub-frequencies include gratitude, joy, relief, contentment, confidence, and well-being. Each person will naturally feel one or more of these sub-frequencies upon being in their new PRL, so there is no need to force gratitude if what you truly feel is relief or joy, for instance. Some people feel thrilled and overflowingly joyous in being in their new reality. Some feel a palpable sense of relief, such as "Finally, this new PRL is mine!". And some feel a deep, calm sense of gratitude and thankfulness for having their heart's desire. Ultimately, only you can know what it feels like to have your heart's desire, but the common thread in all these scenarios is that you are embracing the feeling of ALREADY HAVING and BEING your new PRL.

After you have looped your RHS enough times until it is both sensorily rich and realistic AND you authentically feel that you are experiencing your new PRL here and now, you can fall asleep. As you fall asleep playing the RHS with your new PRL, the new PRL sinks into the heart zone, connected to the divine Eternal Cosmic Library of infinite PRLs. Congratulations, your new PRL is now a reality. The divine mind has started building the Paramorphing Chain which will shift you to your new PRL. It might take a day, a week, or a month, but it doesn't matter. It is done in your inner mind's eye, your sense of I AM, so physical reality will have no choice but to reflect it. Do not worry about the how and when of physical reality. It is unfolding perfectly and from the standpoint of eternity, has already unfolded. So, relax and go about your daily life. If the new PRL comes up in your mind, just gently remind yourself that it is already yours and unfolding perfectly here and now and that the infinitely intelligent divine printer is working 24/7 to breathe physical life into your new PRL, in the most efficient and frictionless way possible. Know that it's done and guaranteed.

One final note is crucial to mention. Do not struggle or try too hard in this process. Paramorphing is about choosing a new PRL calmly and confidently, knowing that all PRLs already exist in God's Eternal Cosmic Library. Doubting or trying too hard generates friction which clogs the divine printer from working optimally. Place your attention and awareness on your chosen RHS scene, but don't fret about whether you are doing the process correctly. This only generates friction. Simply rest in the deep knowing that God gives you desires so you can enjoy them, and that desiring a PRL is only possible if it is already contained with you! Relax, enjoy your chosen RHS scenes, and naturally feel the mixture of positive sentiments that arise while you occupy your new PRL. Then, either wake up refreshed and cheerful, or drift off into sleep. It doesn't matter, although falling asleep in the process of running a RHS often leads to a deep sense of satisfaction and peace when you wake up. Either way, you imprinted the heart zone with your new identity and it will start Paramorphing you to your new PRL in ways your conscious mind cannot possibly fathom.

Disembodying Undesired PRLs

In the last section, we discussed how to embody a desired PRL using the Inside-Out method. Now, we will discuss how to deal with PRLs you deeply dislike or even fear.

The heart's infinitely powerful energy of non-judgmental conviction can be hijacked through the emotion of fear. Fear is not the opposite of love, as many humans mistakenly believe. Fear is absolute conviction in a PRL that you do NOT desire! If you carefully examine your own life, you may notice that your deepest and most pronounced fears often come true. If you truly resent a certain person and never want to see them, you might run into them at the grocery store the very next day. If you deeply fear running out of money, you are demonstrating a palpable conviction in a PRL of poverty and lack and will crystallize that PRL into your physical reality. Fear is simply love wearing a mask. It is the power of love, unfortunately, channeled and misappropriated toward undesired ends. Thus, fear has no real existence or power on its own. Love alone is eternally true and the source of all power.

How does a person combat fear and its powerful grasp on your mind? Resisting fear, stifling it, or pretending fear does not exist will not work. Remember, Paramorphing is the divine law of God, and God is perfectly and absolutely honest. Saying you are not afraid of something, while deep down you are, will not get you anywhere. In fact, resisting something and trying to suppress it will only make it **grow** in strength. The only way to eliminate fear from bringing undesired PRLs into your life is by WHOLLY ACCEPTING that the PRLs you do not desire have a right to exist. Fear thrives in the darkness but withers when you bring it to the light of your I AM awareness. Spiritual masters across the ages have always advised people to face their fears, but Paramorphing explains why and how to actually do it. You can never eliminate anything from God's infinity. Instead, acknowledge it, then reaffirm your identity as a divine child of God, and turn your focus to what you desire.

There are **3 steps** involved in disembodying an undesired or fear-inducing PRL. If there is a PRL which you deeply fear, the **first step** is to courageously look at it straightforwardly. If fear comes up, do not stifle it, but merely observe it, realizing you are the pure I AM in which all PRLs exist. This might be quite difficult depending on how much fear you have toward the PRL. Do not hate, resist, or push it away. Simply see it. Then, wholly ACCEPT that it has a right to exist. Remember, God consists of ALL THINGS. Trying to destroy a particular PRL is equivalent to trying to destroy a piece of God, which can never be done. All things, even those that seem undesirable, cruel, bad, and harmful, have a DIVINE RIGHT to exist in God's Eternal Cosmic Library. In fact, without the existence of the "bad", the "good" would have no meaning. This doesn't mean that you choose these negative PRLs for yourself or allow them into your life. Rather, you neutralize the fear energy that crystallizes them into physical reality by fully and truly accepting that they have a right to exist as POTENTIAL PRLs in God's Eternal Cosmic Library.

Once you have done this, the **second step** is to decide this particular PRL is NOT your choice by doing the exact OPPOSITE of the Inside-Out Method. You may call it the Inverted Inside-Out Method. In the regular Inside-Out Method, we embody a chosen PRL richly and realistically by entering it from a FIRST-PERSON perspective, feeling that we are literally in that reality here and now. We also accessorize our imagined PRL with the 5 senses to lend it a rich sense of realism. In the Inverted Inside-Out Method, we do the opposite. Since we are dealing with a reality that we do NOT want to experience, we view it from the THIRD-PERSON perspective, as an observer looking at a scene from the outside. We also reduce sensory vividness to the bare minimum requirements, so all we need is a black-and-white visual of the scene. Our goal here is to reduce the realism of the scene as much as possible. Sounds, tastes, feelings, and smells are not important. Once you construct the dull, grainy, black-and-white scene, deeply and firmly recognize that this cannot be your chosen reality because you are viewing it from the outside-in. Each time you loop the scene, make it less and less clear until it starts to fade into a hazy gray cloud. Again, we are doing the opposite of the original Inside-Out Method, where we would increase the richness of the scene with each loop. Once your looped scene fades into a dull gray cloud, acknowledge that your undesired reality has now dissolved back into pure potential and will not materialize in your reality.

The **third step** is to use the original Inside-Out method to richly embody a desired PRL in which you experience what you do want. By realistically embodying a PRL in which your fear didn't come true, you turn the power of your attention to what you desire and materialize it. Meanwhile, the reality you formerly feared disappears back into the Eternal Cosmic Library where all PRLs exist as in potential as templates (until emotions magnetize them into physical reality).

Here Is an example of how to realistically disembody a feared PRL. Many people suffer from intrusive thoughts that bother their sense of peace and well-being. For instance, a new mother may dread the prospect of someone at a party dropping and gravely injuring her newborn baby. This can truly be a horrifying thought for any parent, and stifling or resisting it will only cause it to grow in prominence. The solution is to use Paramorphing and the Inverted Inside-Out Method.

The first step would be to accept that there is a PRL in which your baby gets harmed or even fatally injured because someone accidentally dropped him. It may be tremendously difficult to acknowledge and accept that this PRL has a right to exist, but it most certainly does, because ALL PRLs exist in God's Eternal Cosmic Library. The second step is to construct a scene in which someone does drop your baby at the party, but to make it as muted as possible. This is the Inverse Inside-Out Method. Your scene can have dull colors, appear grainy like an old film, or even just be black-and-white. View it from the 3RD-PERSON as an observer looking at a movie. In other words, you should see your full body in the scene, because you are seeing this PRL as an outsider looking in, NOT an active participant. Loop the scene, progressively dulling and muting sensory details with each loop, until your sense of fear and anxiety dissipates as your mental video disappears into a gray or black cloud. Recognize that your unwanted reality has dissolved and will not materialize. Finally, embody your desired PRL richly and realistically. Your desired PRL would obviously be one in which the party has ended successfully, your baby is safe and laughing happily, and you go to bed at night with him safely next to you, so enter this scene using the original Inside-Out Method. You should embody this scene from the FIRST-PERSON perspective, literally feeling the cool bedsheets under you, your baby boy cooing happily next to you, and giggling as you tickle his belly while you smell the baby powder you put on him after the party ended. Let your heart create the appropriate magnetic emotion for this scene, whether it is gratitude, joy, relief, contentment, or some combination of these frequencies. Relish the fact that you have now called and chosen upon your desired PRL, and know with absolute conviction that the undesired PRL has now sunken back into the Eternal Cosmic Library to exist only as latent potential, while the desired PRL that you have richly embodied will materialize in physical reality.

The Outside-In Method

The Inside-Out method focuses on getting to the very core of your being, the infinite I AM, and embodying your new PRL in that suspended twilight state. The Inside-Out method, however, cannot be used during your regular waking consciousness, for obvious reasons. In order to physically crystallize a new PRL, it is important to be as persistent as possible in defining oneself as the new PRL identity. For that reason, it is incredibly helpful to also employ a method during ordinary waking consciousness (the beta brainwave state) to embody the new PRL. In Paramorphing, this is called the Outside-In method, but it is really a collection of techniques and tools that help us "overlay" the desired PRL over our current physical reality, so that the new PRL ultimately displaces our current PRL, first in our imaginative reality, then in physical reality. The Outside-In and Inside-Out methods can be used together and amplify each other; you can use the Outside-In method to mentally stay in your new PRL while awake, and you can use the Inside-Out method to reside in your new PRL while you are resting or about to fall asleep.

The Encyclopedia Technique

The first Outside-In tool is the encyclopedia method. You will script your own biography, your life story, as someone from the future reading about the past, learning about the life that you have already lived. Remember that every possibility, timeline, and lifeline you could ever experience has already been created and exists in God's infinite mind, the Eternal Cosmic Library. Therefore, there is a solid, tangible PRL in which whatever you write down ALREADY exists. Do not be shy or limit yourself. Ask for the whole enchilada, for it is God's good pleasure to give you the full kingdom and to experience Himself through you. Settling is death. Settling is announcing that you are not God and not worthy, which is an illusion borne of false conceptions. The children of the Creator inherently deserve the entire kingdom, and ask with the innocence of little children, knowing that their heavenly Father will not disappoint them.

A handful of people have such a strong, overpowering life mission that they are happy creating a life story with a single item. There is nothing wrong with this. For example, a person might be so utterly sure that their one and only goal in life is to become a platinum-selling music artist who headlines at Glastonbury. Another such person might be utterly sure that their one and only goal in life is to become a billionaire. If that is you, wonderful! There is nothing wrong with being utterly consumed by a single item and defining your life story as such. The fewer the items on your list, the more concentrated and channeled the divine creative energy becomes in Paramorphing you to the PRLs in which your written life story is a physical reality. However, there is no limit to what God can accomplish. The advantage of having fewer items on your list is that it forces you to truly determine your heart's deepest desires and harmonic signature, rather than lukewarm desires imposed on you by others. Most people prefer a life that is rich in multiple dimensions such as health, wealth, and love. What matters is that your life story consists of the life that YOU TRULY want, not what you feel you are "supposed" to experience based on what society, culture, and external factors tell you to experience. Your life story should contain only the experiences that intrinsically make you joyous and make your heart sing; anything else will contain friction that hampers your ability to morph into your desired PRL.

Here is what a sample encyclopedia entry might look like for a young, 27-year-old aspiring pediatrician named Anjali Patel, who learns about Paramorphing and then decides to script her own biography with conviction. Remember, the biography she scripts will not be from the standpoint of her present physical PRL "hoping" for a better "future" (which is an illusion). Anjali will author her encyclopedia entry from the standpoint of already BEING her desired PRL, taking the standpoint of someone 100 years from now looking back and learning about her life. She is not "trying" or "hoping"; she has simply decided the PRL she wishes to embody, and declares I AM that new PRL here and now. She writes her life story accordingly.

1. *Anjali Patel was a world-renowned pediatrician who made pioneering contributions to reducing infant mortality. A research powerhouse, she co-authored over 30 highly impactful scholarly articles in the world's leading medical research journals and also popularized and publicized her research in books that became Sunday Times bestsellers.*

2. *She was also an avid table tennis player and cross-fit enthusiast who hiked on the weekends. Her friends marveled at her energy, joy, and vitality even in her later years, as she left younger hikers trailing!*

3. *Her unusual and original life prescriptions combining modern and traditional healing sciences for youthful living earned her appearances in a number of award-winning popular medical documentaries and even a film that was globally screened.*

4. *Anjali was a devoted mother to 3 beautiful children, who*

found success in different fields and turned out to be well-rounded and kind adults.

5. She enjoyed a lifelong romance with her husband, whom she called her best friend, inspiration, and travel partner. The couple spent their summers in India and enjoyed romantic vacations around the world.

6. The Patel family was a bedrock of the community, deeply involved in school fundraisers, charitable efforts, and fitness initiatives such as the local 5K runs. Friends of the family raved about their close relationship with Anjali and her husband, saying that they were the type of neighbors that everyone dreamed of living nearby. One friend commented how no matter how busy Anjali was with her work and media appearances, she always remained approachable and friendly to all who came to see her, continuing her work as a practicing pediatrician well into her 60s.

7. Anjali Patel lived a full, rich, and absolutely joyful life doing the things she loved and being around those she loved, who loved her in turn. Her life was a blessing in every way.

The PRL in which Anjali has achieved these 7 major bullets or topics already exists in God's divine mind, in which every PRL exists in finished form. By writing her life story in this manner, Anjali is not begging, craving, or hoping, but DECIDING and CHOOSING that this will be her life experience. God's only operative word is YES. The divine mind wishes to experience itself in infinite ways and does not judge. It only grants whatever is asked of it, and when an experience is chosen, it provides the soul with that experience from the Eternal Cosmic Library.

The Reality Draping Technique

The second Outside-In tool is the reality draping technique. It is one of the most potent ways to embody a new PRL and the beauty of this tool is that though it requires imaginative access, it can be done very well in the regular beta-wave waking consciousness, without needing to access the slower theta or alpha states.

Remember, all PRLs, meaning all your infinite lives and timelines, exist right HERE and right NOW. You are the very center of reality, God, looking at himself through one specific vantage point or perspective. Imagine God as an infinitely large sphere. Each point on the sphere is distinct yet also the center of the sphere from its perspective. Likewise, each person is a distinct point of divine consciousness and the center of his reality, though all points are made of the same divine consciousness and the one God. All PRLs are overlaid on top of one another and happen in the timeless present moment, but your belief structure results in you experiencing one specific PRL. You experience a single PRL in 3-dimensional reality, with height, width, and depth. However, ultimate reality, the mind of God, is N-dimensional, meaning every possible sequence of events and experiences you could ever encounter is here and now. It is absolutely impossible to even attempt to understand or process N-dimensions with our 3-dimensional human mind. It would be like a toy car attempting to keep up with racing cars at the Daytona 500. Comical, in short.

While it is impossible to capture N-dimensional reality with 3D models, language, and concepts (the human mind and languages spoken on Earth are all 3D constructs), a good analogy for the nature of PRLs would be nesting dolls. In the same way that a single large nesting doll contains all the other dolls nested within it, though they are invisible from the outside, the present moment contains not only the PRL you experience now but every other PRL as well, though they are hidden from your conscious experience until you choose to Paramorph to them.

This means that each PRL, including any PRL you desire, is "invisibly draped" over your present reality, though you may not perceive it with your physical senses yet. However, by shifting your frame of attention to the desired PRL, instead of your current physical reality, your desired new PRL starts to go from invisible to translucent to eventually a solid, tangible physical reality that displaces your currently experienced PRL, which recedes and dissolves.

In the Inside-Out technique in the prior section, we discussed moving into a semi-conscious twilight state and immersing yourself in the newly desired PRL, moving it into our current experience. In the reality draping technique, we will immerse ourselves in the newly desired PRL by paying attention to the invisible desired PRL, "overlaying" it on top of our present PRL.

For instance, suppose you currently drive a Toyota Camry, but you have clearly decided to Paramorph to a PRL in which you own and drive a Bentley Flying Spur. The point here is not to compare experiences or judge; from God's standpoint, both PRLs are equally meaningful (or meaningless), so it is merely a matter of your choice, rather than a debate on which car and which PRL is "better". Currently, you occupy the "reality skin" of your current PRL, in which you drive a Toyota Camry, and it feels utterly natural and comfortable to you.

Now, you will bring your desired PRL here and now by sitting in your Toyota, but truly FEELING and BELIEVING that you are in your Bentley. Your conscious mind might laugh at you and claim you are being delusional, as would many other people, but it does not matter. There is a PRL in God's Eternal Cosmic Library, here and now, in which you are already driving a Bentley, and you are choosing to breathe life into it. You relax and focus on the UNSEEN PRL which will become as solid and tangible as your SEEN PRL if you can only maintain conviction in the existence of what you desire. You imagine that your hands are grasping a steering wheel with leather grips, mentally "overlaying" the Bentley's steering wheel over the steering wheel you see in your present physical PRL. You imagine seeing a dashboard beautifully crafted with wood finishes, and mentally "overlay" this over the dashboard you see right now. You look at the Toyota symbol on the steering wheel, and in your mind's eye, you overlay the iconic winged Bentley logo over it. You do this with every feature of the car until you are convinced you are not merely pretending or fancying, but LITERALLY DRIVING a Bentley, right here and right now. You must feel the state of being in the new PRL, without pretense. How would you feel about driving a Bentley right now? You might be relieved, satisfied, grateful, thrilled, ecstatic, or smile smugly knowing you sit inside your dream car. Whatever you would naturally feel if you were to physically possess the car, is what you must feel HERE and NOW.

It doesn't matter what your conscious mind says or protests. It was never designed to process infinity, so do not listen too much to its gripes and grumbles. You know in your hearts of hearts, that there is a version of you, already existing in an adjacent PRL, driving that Bentley. By placing your attention and faith in your desired PRL, and claiming it with conviction no matter what your physical reality shows now, the divine mind of God will breathe life into your new PRL. It must. God never judges and only says YES.

This is merely one example of how to drape your desired PRL over your existing physical reality. By removing attention from your current reality, it starts shriveling and receding back into the unmanifested Eternal Cosmic Library, while your attention simultaneously fertilizes and brings to fruition the newly desired PRL that goes from being invisible to tangibly experienced.

Let's take a look at another example. Lisa is a college student who is absolutely enamored with Henry, a doctoral student in her school's Ph.D. program whom she deeply admires and wants to marry. Lisa and Henry spoke briefly last year, and sparks flew, leading to a few dates, but things fizzled out afterward. Since then, Lisa has tried everything to regain Henry's attention and affection, including signing up for his recitation, but to no avail.

Frustrated, Lisa realizes that she has been trying to manipulate her existing PRL with crude physical force, instead of simply Paramorphing to the new PRL in which she is already in a happy relationship with Henry. Now, to an external observer, the things that Lisa does might seem "delusional", but it doesn't matter; to Paramorph to any PRL, you must believe in its existence before you have any physical sensory proof for it. Your physical reality is your shadow and merely follows you. It cannot transform until you transform your inner identity, who you are conscious of being, and who you say I AM.

Lisa happily goes to bed each night, truly feeling that Henry is cuddling her in bed. She holds a pillow and falls asleep holding it each night, feeling it is Henry. While an external observer might remark that it is merely a pillow, to Lisa, it is certainly not; she is hugging Henry. As she goes about her day, Lisa feels Henry is around her in her living room and kitchen and says phrases like "What do you want for dinner, Henry?", focusing on the currently invisible but very real PRL in which he is at her place. She even opens up a text simulator app on her phone and creates a realistic-looking text exchange between her and Henry which tells her he loves her, written in his natural and characteristically sarcastic style. Lisa reads this text a couple of times a day, fully aware that there is a PRL in which this text message from Henry already exists because if she could imagine it, there is a PRL where it is a physical reality! She also decides that she is tired of pedestalizing another person and starts pedestalizing the divinity inside, her inner I AM that decides and chooses instead of begging and craving. During the day, Lisa doesn't consciously think about Henry, but when he pops up in her mind, she smiles happily and gratefully about the fact that he is hers and that they are in a relationship. However, she doesn't obsess over him or put her life on hold. She spends the vast majority of the day doing things she loves, advancing in her career, making new friends, and prioritizing her own joy instead of pining. What is there to pine for? Lisa believes, with absolute faith, that her inner sense of I AM and the PRL she has chosen imaginatively is her true causal reality. She also trusts her higher, supremely intelligent God-mind, linked to the Eternal Cosmic Library of all PRLs, to Paramorph her to her newly desired reality through a perfect and optimally efficient Paramorphing Chain. She also moves to the conviction that everything is unfolding ideally around her.

For a few weeks, seemingly nothing changes in Lisa's physical reality. At this point, she could complain, gripe, and doubt whether Paramorphing is real, or persist even more strongly in knowing that she is in her new PRL, no matter what her physical reality displays right now. A few weeks later, when she is thoroughly enjoying herself and living her best life, she suddenly gets a text message from a friend inviting her to a party. She goes there sees that Henry is also there, and in fact learns that he was the one who invited her. He confesses that, for reasons unknown to him, he has been thinking about her for the past several weeks. His mother even gifted him a sweater that reminded him of Lisa, because she enjoyed wearing the same brand. Henry sheepishly admits that he likes her and asks her out on a date, and curiously, he actually said one of the EXACT lines that Lisa had envisioned him saying to her and written down in her text simulator app. It turns out that the Paramorphing Chain had worked mysteriously and powerfully in the background, subtly prompting Henry to think of Lisa and grow attracted to her in ways her conscious mind could have never fathomed.

This isn't unusual for those who understand Paramorphing. The reality in which Lisa and Henry are together exists FOREVER in God's Eternal Cosmic Library. Lisa wasn't creating this PRL or changing/convincing Henry. She wasn't manipulating him, infringing on his free will, or "controlling his mind". The PRL in which Henry doesn't like her exists, as does the PRL in which Henry likes her, in addition to an infinite number of alternative PRLs with different relationships between Lisa and Henry, ranging from bitter enemies to neutral classmates to passionately married lovers. Lisa wasn't trying to destroy other PRLs but merely watered her desired PRL of a romantic relationship until that reality blossomed into physical fruition. All other possibilities then receded back into the invisible Eternal Cosmic Library where all PRLs lie in dormant potential until they are summoned into physical crystallization. The PRL in which Lisa is not with Henry also exists, but Lisa no longer sees and experiences this because her attention is no longer on it.

Once she picked her new desired PRL and stuck firmly to it while pedestalizing herself as the sole creator of her destiny, the infinite divine intelligence seamlessly Paramorphed her into her new reality by orchestrating the movement of a thousand hidden levers in perfect harmony, invisibly yet efficiently directing people and circumstances. Your conscious mind can never possibly understand the infinite intelligence of God, so stop trying to fathom the exact process and steps involved in transforming your physical reality. The Lord, I AM, confirms this in the Book of Isaiah: "As the heavens are higher than the earth, so are my ways higher than your ways". Simply move internally to your new PRL, embody it faithfully, and leave the rest to God, the N-dimensional infinite intelligence in which "we live and move and have our being".

The Confirmation Benefit Technique

Psychologists in the 20th and 21st centuries have spent much time researching so-called decision biases and heuristics that they have labeled to be problematic impediments to making "rational decisions". However, what they do not recognize is that there is no such thing as objective reality or evidence, only circumstances and PRLs that come into being depending on the observer. Each PRL has a corresponding observer, and vice versa. If a PRL is focused on and believed to be true, it will start crystallizing into physical reality, no matter what the "rational" conscious mind deems to be possible or logical.

One of the most well-known and well-researched psychological phenomena is confirmation bias, the tendency to favor, notice, and seek out evidence that supports our belief structure while disregarding evidence that contradicts it. Psychologists on earth, however, have made the flaw of assuming there is a single objective reality. There are infinite PRLs, and infinite realms of experience, with a corresponding belief structure that creates each. Therefore, in Paramorphing, when a person adopts a belief structure with conviction, he moves to a PRL in which those beliefs are necessarily true and reflected in his physical reality. There is no objective truth in PRLs, for the only objective truth is I AM, the pure God-consciousness in which all PRLs exist eternally.

That is why this third technique is called Confirmation Benefit rather than Confirmation Bias. What you see, notice, and believe becomes your PRL. Now, this goes far beyond what most humans can fathom. Most people have preliminarily accepted the idea that the RAS (Reticular Activating System) in the brain acts as a sort of reality filter. According to neurological research, the RAS explains why, for instance, thinking about red cars makes you notice red cars on the road. According to RAS explanations, there is still only one objective reality, but you happen to notice different parts of it based on your focus; in other words, according to most RAS theories, there is only one reality that has cars of every color, but you become aware of the red ones once you pay attention to that particular color.

Paramorphing goes far beyond this and reveals the whole truth, which can be difficult for the logical mind to accept and can only be proven via personal experience. In Paramorphing, putting your attention on red cars literally moves you to a separate universe, a new PRL in which there are more red cars. Now, due to sensory consistency and memory, it might seem like you are merely in one reality that happens to be changing, but in truth, there are infinite PRLs of every gradient imaginable. There are PRLs in which cars on the road are evenly distributed in color, PRLs in which red is a slightly popular choice, and yes, even PRLs in which every car on the road is red. Of course, you most likely don't see that final PRL because your predominant belief structure, if you are like most people, is that people buy cars in an assortment of colors. However, by focusing on the color red, and aligning with it, you Paramorph to nearby PRLs in which slightly more cars are red compared to your existing PRL. It appears to just be a "coincidence" or you merely "noticing more red cars", but you may have very well shifted to an entirely new physical reality, a PRL in which everything else in your environment is essentially the same except car colors, which are now more likely to be red. In other words, it isn't you merely noticing different aspects of one physical reality; you might have actually Paramorphed to an entirely new physical reality universe altogether since infinite potential PRLs exist.

Of course, proving any of this would be beyond the scope of this book, and not fully possible even with the most advanced science and mathematics on earth. The good news, however, is that Paramorphing is not concerned with the how and when. God's ways of bringing a PRL to pass in physical reality are done with N-dimensional infinite intelligence, something which is impossible for the 3-dimensional human mind, logic, and language to grasp. God simply decrees and becomes a chosen reality. Thus, simply apply and test the technique for yourself, and monitor the results you receive, and you will be left with no doubt that you are hopping from one PRL to another. Who cares if people object to your convictions or call you delusional when you suddenly find yourself blessed by seemingly miraculous health, wealth, love, and success in life? If you practice the techniques of Paramorphing and magically seem to find solutions and resolutions for challenges in your life that previously seemed unsolvable, who cares whether others find it "logically plausible"?

To execute the Confirmation Benefit technique, simply write down the details of your desired PRL and consciously start only focusing on pieces of evidence that support your desired PRL. If you notice circumstances or evidence contrary to your new PRL or reflective of your old or existing PRL, simply ignore them and label them as part of a reality that is no longer your choice. All possible PRLs already exist, but by selectively and persistently placing your attention on your desired PRL, you channel the divine, non-judgmental energy of God to breathe life into it.

Let us take the example of Jason, an electrician struggling with debt and unable to pay rent or put food on the table for his family, including his 1-year-old daughter. Jason's wife, Rebecca, tries her very best to find work, but to no avail. The family has less than a few months of savings before they face homelessness, so Jason decides to stop fighting his existing PRL of poverty and simply Paramorph to a new PRL of affluence and comfortable living. Jason's wife agrees that she desires to move to this new PRL as well, so the couple sits down and creates a shared spreadsheet with the details of their new PRL. They discuss their truest and deepest heart's desires and write down the following items: Abundant and effortless monthly cashflow to comfortably afford rent and groceries, a home of their own, and a loving babysitter who takes excellent care of their daughter, at an affordable hourly rate, so Jason and Rebecca can work peacefully at high-paying jobs.

Jason and Rebecca look at the spreadsheet each morning with gladness and gratitude, and also lovingly look at the spreadsheet before going to bed each night. A week later, Rebecca receives a message from an online survey company offering to pay her $50 for a 15-minute survey. She scoffs at the amount, which wouldn't even be enough to buy a week's worth of groceries, let alone pay for rent. However, Jason reminds her to faithfully trust the law of Paramorphing and notes down the $50 in their spreadsheet. In his state of total conviction, it is tangible evidence of their new PRL of abundant monthly cash flow. Rebecca, though still not satisfied, writes it down.

Another week passes, and it is now Jason's turn to start to grow mildly frustrated. The couple has barely a month's worth of savings left before they are evicted from their apartment. However, Rebecca urges Jason to stay convinced in their new PRL because she has witnessed small miracles over the last week. An old and wealthy friend of hers, whom Rebecca hadn't seen for years, dropped by their apartment and gave a $500 gift card for the baby. Rebecca also met Sharon, a stay-at-home mom in a nearby housing development who said she was making excellent money from home by providing copywriting and digital advertising services. It turned out that her company needed another junior digital analyst, so she offered to introduce Rebecca to the hiring manager. Rebecca didn't even ask; Sharon just offered, which, once again, appeared to Rebecca to be evidence of a higher power.

Two weeks later, Jason received the news that his elderly aunt had a heart attack and was rushed to the hospital. Although he was never particularly close with her, Rebecca intuitively felt it would be good for Jason to visit her in person since the hospital was only a few miles from their home, so the couple headed out.

While waiting to see his aunt, Jason overhears a few medical imaging specialists at a nearby desk talking about a staffing shortage. Intrigued, Jason naturally felt an inclination to walk up to them and ask what was going on. The specialists explained that 2 staff electricians had unexpectedly quit in the last week, leading to major issues in running critical hospital functions including the ICUs. Immediately, Jason offered to help, explaining that he was a professional electrician looking for work. While the hiring process would have ordinarily taken weeks, the medical imaging specialists decided to make a rare exception to expedite the process and hire Jason the very next week, at an hourly rate far above average since there was a critical need for the role.

While visiting his aunt in her room, Jason noticed another girl in the room. Her aunt explained that this was her daughter's friend who was in town for the summer and needed a place to stay. Rebecca immediately offered to let the girl stay at their apartment, if she could help take care of their baby when Jason and Rebecca were out of the house. The girl agreed right away.

A week later, Sharon phoned Rebecca, congratulating her on being selected for the new digital advertising position.

Jason and Rebecca never let up their faith, and while it seemed to be a close call, the divine mind of God had Paramorphed them into their new reality in perfect timing. Now, they both had high-paying jobs with bountiful cash flow, more than enough to pay rent and live an affluent life. They had a wonderful babysitter to take care of their daughter. And a year later, when Jason's elderly aunt passed away, Jason learned that she had been so moved by his visit while she was bedridden in the hospital, that she left him a quarter-million dollars. Rebecca knew that this was God's way of giving them the downpayment they needed to buy a home of their own.

All the while, Jason and Rebecca lived in their desired PRL and noted ONLY the things that confirmed their new reality. When struggles, challenges, hardships, and doubts popped up, they simply dismissed them as artifacts of an old and defunct PRL that no longer applied to them. Each day, they wrote down one thing, no matter how small, that confirmed the emergence and crystallization of their newly desired PRL in their spreadsheet. And it appeared. It had to.

There is also a more general version of the Confirmation Benefit technique that can work for those who currently struggle to believe in and seek evidence for a specific new PRL. The general version helps to build belief in the possibility of Paramorphing to other PRLs because you can only perceive what you can believe. **Remember, there are PRLs, parallel versions of Earth, in which humans drink poison without dying like Shiva, bring the dead back to life as Jesus did with Lazarus, and fly like Hanuman.** However, if you firmly believe that such abilities are "paranormal" and "impossible", you will never see those worlds! Now, on the other hand, you don't need to leap from your present set of beliefs to a vastly different PRL. Start by consciously acknowledging how feats that you take to be common today, such as sending an Ultra-HD video to a person on the other side of the world in seconds, would have been seen as delusional to the average human in 1950, clinically insane to someone living in 1900, and pure sorcery or fantasy to someone in 1850. The idea that the average person could cross the ocean from New York to Paris in a few hours on a flying machine called an airplane would have seemed magical and nonsensical to a person in the Middle Ages whose belief structure could not see a PRL beyond ships and sea voyages. Humans believed that running a 4-minute mile was impossible until Roger Bannister accomplished the feat; today there are high schoolers who have run a 4-minute mile. When tennis legend Roger Federer won his 20th Grand Slam, the world was sure the monumental feat could never be eclipsed; yet, within 5 years, fellow tennis legends Rafael Nadal and Novak Djokovic both eclipsed Federer's record. In the world of strongman sports, Eddie Hall deadlifted a seemingly unthinkable 500 kilograms; shortly after, fellow strongman Hafthor Bjornsson matched the feat. If you can go from believing that a 500-kilogram deadlift is impossible to accepting it as a realistic human capability, you can also move to the PRL in which a person channels enough energy to lift a mountain like Krishna did with Govardhan Hill. It is merely a matter of your degree of belief pertaining to the domain of human strength. If you formerly believed that humans could not live past 70, which was a firmly held belief for most people who lived through the disease-stricken Middle Ages, and then learned about the 112-year-old American WW2 veteran Richard Overton, you could just as easily move to a PRL where people live for thousands of years like the great spiritual master Mahavatar Babaji, for that PRL exists as well, though it remains invisible to you until you bring it within your belief structure. Your beliefs are the sole determinant of your witnessed physical world, which is merely one PRL template that the divine printer projects into physical reality based on your truest and deepest beliefs.

The specific record or domain of achievement is not our focus here; what matters is the fact that human beliefs can grow infinitely and physically materialize a correspondingly infinite number of PRLs with possibilities and capabilities that could previously not be fathomed.

To employ the generalized version of the Confirmation Benefit technique, simply write down these **7 Magical Paramorphing Mantras** in a spreadsheet or notebook, and start noting confirmatory evidence right away. The 7 mantras here are infused with a tremendous amount of spiritual heart zone power that can Paramorph you to a vast array of PRLs in God's Eternal Cosmic Library. You will be pleasantly surprised at the tiny miracles that start popping up in your life, and if you continue at it long enough, you will start seeing massive changes that will unmistakably confirm that you have Paramorphed to new PRLs where all your heart's desires come true. Read these mantras multiple times a day, write or type them out, or simply mentally dwell on them. For an added potency boost, you can even record them and listen to them while you are falling asleep or in the "twilight state" discussed in the prior chapter. The results will speak for themselves.

The 7 Magical Paramorphing Mantras

1. I live a charmed life that overflows with power, abundance, love, joy, and fortune.

2. I am an eternally beloved and divinely royal Child of God whom everyone prioritizes.

3. God lovingly illuminates my life with the most beautiful gifts, surprises, and miracles.

4. It feels so sparkling, energizing, and heartwarming to be The Chosen One.

5. All my pursuits perfectly flower, ripen, and blossom into glorious victory.

6. My heart's deepest and most burning desires flow to me magically and magnetically.

7. It is truly wonderful to know that my wishes are already mine and granted to me freely.

* * * * * * * * * *

Chapter 7: Questions and Answers

The 6 chapters above cover everything you need to know in order to Paramorph successfully into any PRL you choose. Your entire life is a choice, a particular PRL that you consciously or unconsciously believe yourself to be and therefore experience as your physical reality. When you change your inner conception of self, linking the infinitely divine I AM in your heart zone to a new PRL, the infinite intelligence of the divine printer gradually and imperceptibly moves countless levers to subtly Paramorph you into your new PRL in a perfectly efficient manner. Your conscious mind merely decides on a destination with conviction, like a passenger buying a train ticket to a new city. You then sit back, relax, and allow the higher divine mind in your heart zone to move you along the perfect Paramorphing Chain of intermediary PRLs to arrive at your new PRL, in the same way that a passenger on a train doesn't try to move the train himself (how ludicrous!) but simply trusts and allows the vehicle to carry him to his intended destination.

In the introduction, I made the promise that this would be a short work because the mechanics of Paramorphing are extremely simple. In fact, if you have absolute trust and pure, childlike faith, you could simply decree a new PRL and move to it without needing to know anything else. The story of the great saint and spiritual master Prahlad is a perfect example. Prahlad's father was a demon king who wished to torment his son and even kill him, sentencing him to death in the cruelest ways possible, yet Prahlad's perfect faith in God's protective love saved him each time, without fail. The density of the earthly realm makes perfect, pure, and unquestioning childlike faith nearly impossible except in the rarest cases of saints, wizards, and mystics, but everyone can develop faith in their infinite internal capabilities by gradually applying Paramorphing to their lives and reaping the benefits.

Each time you Paramorph into a new PRL, no matter how subtle or small the shift is compared to your prior PRL, you are proving that you are the God of your experienced physical reality and the architect of your world, projecting it from your imagined state of who you truly feel you are. As you gain trust and confidence in your own creative powers, friction will reduce, and you will find yourself rapidly leaping to progressively "greater" PRLs. In the domain of eating, for instance, there are people who barely have any appetite at all; people who have healthy appetites; competitive eaters who can eat dozens of pounds of food in a sitting; humans like Guinness World Record holder Michel Lotito, who regularly consumed metal and glass for years and remained healthy after eating an entire airplane; and mystics like Trailanga Swami who could drink gallons of poisonous substances like quicklime without any ill effects whatsoever. Each of these PRLs, and countless others, exists eternally. The point, of course, is not to endorse eating pounds of food, airplanes, or bleach merely because it can be done. The point is to demonstrate that from God's cosmic vantage point, there is inherently nothing "amazing" or "more worthy" about being able to do "normal" feats like eating a plum versus "abnormal" feats like eating glass. If you truly believe in a particular PRL, it must appear. Whether you believe you are barely musically gifted enough to play at a local bar, or talented enough to sell out Radio City Music Hall, the divine printer will say "Yes, you are correct!" and breathe life into the corresponding physical reality. The PRLs you genuinely embody and feel yourself to be inexorably create your life.

I have personally seen people achieve marvelous results and completely transform their lives by applying Paramorphing. In this final section, I have aggregated and grouped together some of the most common (and insightful) questions I have personally received, seen, and heard from countless people of different ages, genders, races, nationalities, abilities, beliefs, and religious backgrounds. The ultimate beauty of Paramorphing is that it contains universally true answers regardless of who asks the questions or what the questions are about. For this reason, reading through this final chapter will help consolidate the core themes of Paramorphing and fill in any missing gaps or doubts that might have arisen as you read through the first 6 chapters.

This all seems so wild. I feel a bit dizzy just thinking about the fact that I am creating my entire reality and that I have somehow chosen everything in my life. What is the point? It is all a bit overwhelming, to be honest.

The point is that you are God, the pure I AM that always exists, and you are experiencing yourself in an infinite number of ways. I AM is complete, whole, and unchanging, but limits itself in an infinite number of ways to access an infinite number of experiences. If you stayed as God, in the state of all-that-is, you wouldn't be able to experience anything because God is both the experience and the things that are experienced. You had to forget your innate divinity when you became a human so you could richly and realistically experience the PRL of being a human. You have been dreaming, thinking you are a small, powerless, and limited creature when you are actually God, the supreme creator. For whatever reason, you have now come across Paramorphing, the ancient master science that functions like an alarm clock in your dream telling you to wake up. You now know that you can truly have or be anything you desire. Whether you faithfully trust and act on this, or stay asleep, is wholly your choice. Your free will in choosing PRLs is the sole determinant that governs your reality.

Is there anything wrong with staying asleep and dreaming instead of waking up, so to speak?

Of course not! Every PRL, every experience, is rich and valid. In fact, some souls may decide to have entire lives where they commit to not waking up, just so they get a rich and realistic experience of pain and suffering. You might find this insane from a human standpoint, but from your higher self's vantage point, there is nothing inherently better about the PRL in which you are a handsome billionaire compared to the PRL in which you are unattractive and impoverished. Your higher self, which is one with God, knows that you are unconditionally loved, perfect, luminous, unblemished, infinitely attractive, and glorious beyond description, so all flavors of experience are to be cherished. For whatever reason, Paramorphing has now stumbled into your hands. I cannot say why. Perhaps it is because you chose, "before" you entered this current lifetime, to endure a certain series of experiences and then get a wake-up call so you could learn how to consciously craft your reality. Regardless of the reason, you now have the tools to completely overhaul your experienced reality, but even if you don't, you are still a beloved and unblemished child of God. You can always choose to "play the game" of earth, as many times as you wish, and wear countless masks, experiencing an infinite array of PRLs with different degrees of awareness regarding who you truly are. In the end, it truly doesn't matter. All that Paramorphing offers you is a chance to obtain all your burning heart's desires in this lifetime if you choose to do so.

Why does each person have a different heart's Harmonic Signature? For example, I dream of being a world-famous opera singer who performs at the Met (Metropolitan Opera House) while I couldn't care less about being a billionaire tech mogul; on the other hand, many of the people who come to listen to me are solely obsessed with the idea of running business empires but couldn't care less about achieving musical fame. Why?

God seeks to explore his infinitude in an infinite number of ways. Each atom in existence has its own perception of infinity from its unique vantage point. Each person is God, the whole, looking at himself from one "angle", if you will, forgetting that he is in fact, the whole. You believe yourself to be a person looking at an external world, when in reality your body, your possessions, and the entire external world you perceive are merely a projection of your mind. Your Harmonic Signature, your truest and deepest desires, represent the portion of infinity that God wishes to experience through YOUR physical form. Even if your awareness is presently on a version of you that deeply desires to be a famous opera singer, there are infinite parallel versions of you, including PRLs in which you only desire to be a tech mogul, for instance. Likewise, there are infinite parallel versions of the people who come to see you perform, including PRLs in which they only want to be opera singers and don't care about business. However, your awareness is CURRENTLY in a PRL in which you desire operatic fame, and those others desire business success. In this present PRL, you simply know in your heart of hearts that operatic stardom is what will fill you with gladness and joy. You could, of course, choose to not pursue it, but why? Why not do the things and act in the ways that will fill you with joy and love? Your heart's desires are God overtly hinting at what will most truly fulfill you in this lifetime. It would be wise to listen when God nudges you.

If everything I see is just a PRL that my own mind projects, do other people exist? Or are they all just thought forms that exist in my mind? Is there anyone else out there or just me?

God is ONE, but that oneness seeks to explore himself in infinite ways through infinite points of consciousness. So, while you are a child of God, an infinitely capable point of divine consciousness, all other humans (and animals and other creatures) are also unique points of the one divine consciousness. However, the VERSION of those other people, creatures, and forms that you perceive depends on your chosen PRL. Remember, all PRLs exist eternally. There are PRLs in which people around you hate you and PRLs in which they adore you. There are PRLs in which your spouse admires and respects you, PRLs in which you endure the quiet desperation of a poor marriage, and PRLs in which you are amicably divorced. Every version of your spouse already exists in a separate PRL, but it is YOUR conception of who you say I AM that determines which PRL materializes in your physical reality. Other people are points of consciousness, divine children of God just like you, but you only experience the portion of their infinitude that resonates and corresponds with what you authentically feel yourself to be. This means that you can never change anyone; you can only change yourself, and accordingly see the changed version of other people that matches your newly transformed state. You, in short, are the master key to changing anything, the Alpha and the Omega.

What does this mean for relationships? Do others have no free will? If I want to change something about a particular person, is that possible? Can I get someone to fall in love with me? Can I get people who have despised me to admire, adore, respect, and prioritize me?

You are never changing anyone. You are simply moving to the PRL in which a given person ALREADY EXISTS in the form that you desire. For example, suppose you have a turbulent relationship with your father, whom you find to be overly demanding and unappreciative. You must recognize that you can never change this version of him, for the PRL in which he is demanding and unsupportive will always exist eternally. Fighting it or trying to eliminate this PRL is impossible because God's Eternal Cosmic Library consists of all PRLs! In fact, trying to eliminate a PRL is equal to trying to delete a piece of God, an act which can never succeed and in fact, will generate intense friction and reinforce your undesired reality. This is the reason why hating or despising something draws it more intensely into your life. The solution is to ACCEPT that every PRL has a right to exist, and then summon your desired PRL and Paramorph into it. With regards to your father, in this case, there is already an existing PRL in which your father cherishes and supports you in every way. Employ the Paramorphing techniques to embody this new PRL here and now, without fighting or complaining about your existing PRL, and magic will unfold. You will move to experiencing the PRL with the version of him that is kind, loving, and supportive, for if you can imagine it, it exists!

Similarly, suppose you desire to marry a girl who currently does not appear to be interested in you. As a Paramorpher, you know that all PRLs exist here and now, including the PRL in which this particular girl is already married to you. Therefore, start embodying and BEING in that PRL here and now. Assume that you are married to this girl HERE and NOW, knowing that you are calling forth that particular PRL from the Eternal Cosmic Library of latent potential into your physical reality. **You are not coercing, harming, or forcing someone else against their free will; this would be a grave mistake because every PRL has a right to exist, including the PRL in which that girl does not want you.** Never forcefully violate a person's free will. Simply allow that possible PRL to exist, while internally moving to the PRL in which you are married to the version of her that wants you and chooses you of her own free will. Remember, whenever you see a person, you are merely seeing ONE possible version of them out of an INFINITE number of versions of them that exist in the Eternal Cosmic Library. Your 3D senses fool you into thinking people are solid, unchanging, and homogeneous entities, but your physical reality is merely one crystallized possibility that emerged from a field of INFINITE possibilities.

I know my father well, so I could see this happening, but what about getting someone famous to fall in love with me? I have a crush on a well-known singer from a globally recognized band. Are you saying that there is a PRL in which I am together with that man? Can I actually move to that reality?

Of course, such a PRL exists. With God, all things are possible. It doesn't matter whether you desire $5 or $5 million, the barista who works at your local coffee shop, or a world-famous celebrity. In your reality, YOU ALONE are the decider, and you alone possess the divine power to move to any PRL you choose. Now, keep in mind that others have their own realities and can shape them perfectly based on their free will. You can only shape your own reality, but the beauty is because you have full and total access to the Eternal Cosmic Library of all PRLs, you can choose and move to any PRL you desire, including one where you are married to that particular famous singer.

The catch, if you will, is never in the circumstances, but in your own internal friction in moving to such a PRL. Are you absolutely convinced that you are the God of your experienced reality and that your heart zone can Paramorph you to any PRL? If so, it most certainly will happen. However, if you doubt whether it is possible, secretly dismiss it as a pipedream or a fantasy, or give up on your newly desired PRL at the first sign of difficulty, you will generate intense friction that congests the divine printer and prevents it from breathing life into the reality that you desire. If doubts and difficulties emerge, you can consult Chapter 5, which thoroughly explains how to totally eliminate any kind of friction. However, the most fundamental route to eliminating friction is to deeply and wholly understand and trust, in your heart and bones, that you are I AM, God in human form, and that all PRLs are already given to you to experience and enjoy. Jesus called the Eternal Cosmic Library the Kingdom of Heaven. It is already yours. Only your pedestalization, doubt, or disbelief of a particular desired PRL can hamper its physical materialization.

What if I don't know what I truly want? I'm not sure exactly what career will make me happy, or what my heart's Harmonic Signature is. I feel the same about relationships. I don't know exactly what I want my boyfriend to look like or where to even search for the perfect person. How can I move to desirable PRLs when I don't have a precise sense of clarity around what I want?

Earth is a unique realm of experience, which offers the soul the opportunity to play the game of life in "expert mode". This doesn't necessarily mean that life here has to be hard; it simply means that greater conviction and intentional force are required to mold reality as you see fit and Paramorph to new PRLs. As we have discussed, in other realms and universes, even casual thoughts can quickly and easily produce grand results in one's experienced physical reality. For instance, a person on certain higher astral realms and heavens may wish to see a glorious nature scape with a crystal waterfall and bioluminescent plants and find it materializing into his experienced reality in a split second. On Earth, the soul truly learns how to persist in a desired reality until it materializes, a lesson that cannot be learned as deeply in other realms.

Why do you want the things that you want? Because you know, deep in your heart, that you will feel immense gladness, peace, and joy upon receiving them. Earth is the learning ground where one learns to truly listen to the heart's Harmonic Signature. Because Paramorphing to new PRLs on Earth requires persistent conviction, the soul learns how to prioritize desires. You do not need to know your dream partner's specific physical features, for instance. Yet, you DO know how you would **FEEL** to be in the PRL in which you are together. Envision it right now using the Outside-In technique. Imagine you have your perfect husband or boyfriend lying in bed next to you, as you rest your head on his chest while he softly strokes your hair (if this is what you want). How do you feel? Perhaps you will feel warmth and joy. Maybe you will finally feel a deep and palpable sense of relief that you are in a relationship. And perhaps you will feel an inexplicable mixture of emotions that can't be easily put into words. That's totally fine. What matters is that you experience the PRL of already having your perfect partner here and now. You can even literally verbalize it by expressing your gratitude as a repetitive mantra such as "I am so thankful that I am now married to a man who is absolutely perfect for me in every way", while truly feeling this new PRL. Remember, it is never the method or technique that matters. You are a child of God, an embodiment of the infinite Creator. What matters is that you earnestly develop the consciousness of "I AM IN MY NEW PRL NOW", no matter how contrary to that desired PRL your present physical reality appears. The same is true if you don't know how much money you want to earn, for example. You DO know what it feels like to have enough money to pay for all your expenses, buy beautiful clothes for your children, comfortably afford dinners at nice restaurants, and enjoy a basic sense of peace and well-being that you are financially secure. Capture this feeling deeply and when you do so, you will breathe life into a new PRL where you make exactly the necessary amount of money that allows you to afford and enjoy all the things you have imagined experiencing.

How can we tell if we are embodying our new PRL the "right way"? How can I tell if I'm Paramorphing correctly? There seems to be no way to definitively see if I'm on track. Are there signs we can look for, or is it possible to get hints from the universe in some way? What about synchronicities?

There is most certainly a way to see if you're on track. In fact, it is the only way to see if you're on track. How do you FEEL? Who are YOU conscious of being, here and now? That is the only true benchmark of the physical reality that you will soon be experiencing. Whatever you say I AM, and truly believe yourself to be, is the PRL template that will crystallize into your life experience. Once you are internally conscious of being in your new PRL, in your imagination, that is all the proof you need. **In fact, you alone can be the judge of whether you are doing things correctly, so first move to the foundational assumption that you are God, you are the basis of reality, and everything you do or don't do is moving you in perfect harmony toward your new PRL.** Once you rest in the loving conviction of already being in your newly desired PRL here and now, all your actions (or lack thereof) become magically infused with a Midas touch. If you do take an action? It is perfect. If you don't take an action? It is perfect also. Once you establish the top of the Paramorphing Pyramid (imaginatively BEING your new PRL), whatever emotions, thoughts, and actions you take will work out beautifully and it will appear that you can do no wrong. If you do NOT imaginatively assert yourself to already be your new PRL here and now, or doubt you can morph into your new PRL, nothing you feel, think, or do will matter or work out. BEING, or I AM is the God in you. As the Book of Matthew teaches, once you have sought the Kingdom of

Heaven in you, all other things shall be added unto you. The Kingdom of Heaven is your inner sense of I AM. Once you prioritize your own inner light and become conscious of embodying the PRL you wish to experience, your emotions, thoughts, and actions will flow perfectly from your state of being. They will be effortlessly added to you. God, after all, is irresistible!

Now, once you have established your awareness of being in a new PRL, you may get wonderful and perfectly customized hints that your new PRL is coming to life. Yes indeed! These synchronicities can be exciting and thrilling, and they will often carry meaning for you alone while others might dismiss them as coincidences. It doesn't matter. Above all, though, know that the surest sign or synchronicity is your internal conviction of being in your new PRL, no matter what. This trumps everything else.

Honestly, I know deep down in my gut that Paramorphing must be true. I can intuitively sense that the entire world is an illusion and that everything is created from thought or imagination. I also feel that I am a child of God and that a loving God would not deny his children anything. Yet, I still find my mind protesting and arguing. It seems to tell me, "No! It can't be that easy!". It is almost as if my mind feels that life necessarily needs to be a battle and a struggle and that things are only achieved through hard work and luck. The idea that I am actually in control of my entire reality and can transform it 100% is something I want to believe, but my mind rebels defiantly. It is really hard to believe that I can be and have anything my heart desires.

It is somewhat natural for many people on Earth to feel this way, given the density of the realm. In other realms, the relationship between one's self-conception and experienced reality is obvious and unmistakable. If you wished for more money and a bag of silver dollars instantly appeared in your hand, you would be absolutely confident in knowing that you are the Creator God of your entire reality. Earth, however, is a realm in which the materialization of a chosen PRL takes time, focus, conviction, and persistence, leading people to believe that there are factors outside of their control that can influence their reality. However, despite the Earth's density, the fundamental truth of BEING still applies because it is the only absolute truth in the entire universe. Your entire physical reality, the PRL you experience, is solely and exclusively a function of your conception of who you are, who you genuinely say and feel I AM.

The only way to truly and deeply know this is to embrace your creative power consciously and start applying Paramorphing, not here and there, but in EVERY moment. Paramorphing is not just one of many things that you can think about and pursue; it is the foundational science of life, the universe, and your entire experienced reality. Make it the cornerstone of your life. While you can access ANY PRL, you are likely to have more friction toward PRLs that involve constraints on time and space. For instance, suppose you wanted natural fame and acclaim as a flutist, and you currently play the flute at a reasonably advanced but not expert level. The PRL in which you headline a solo flute performance at Carnegie Hall next month exists, but you are likely to have friction in attempting to embody that PRL immediately. The goal itself, playing at Carnegie Hall, may seem daunting to you, and the time constraint of being ready to perform by next month may be even more daunting still. Therefore, remove the friction-inducing time and space factors by simply declaring your new PRL to be "I played before a sold-out crowd at Carnegie Hall that relished my performance". Don't mandate the how and the when of your newly desired PRL, which can cause friction. Simply embody your new PRL internally, use the Paramorphing practical application methods, and the Paramorphing Chain will provide the appropriate links, in ways your conscious mind could not ever fathom, to efficiently take you to your desired PRL.

Apart from your "grander" goals, ensure that you closely observe how you are creating your reality every moment. If there is someone you do not get along with, visualize them as just a tad more cheerful, and observe what happens. You might have friction toward visualizing an annoying coworker as a best friend, but you probably can envision them being 5% nicer to you or giving you a compliment in front of your team, for example. If you have perfect faith, you can even Paramorph to a reality where a bitter enemy apologizes to you and becomes a trusted friend.

You have mentioned that we can Paramorph to any PRL and that the only factor that can prevent this is friction. But what about things we consider to be scientific facts such as the law of gravity, human aging, and the seasons?

You can defy gravity and fly. Saints and mystics have done it, but if your present belief structure views that as a ludicrous impossibility or myth, you will never experience it. You can walk on water, quite literally, like Jesus, and part the seas, like Moses. You can defy the human aging process and retain youthful immortality like the eternally youthful Mahavatar Babaji. You can command the skies to rain and they will, and order the sun to stop rising, and it will cease to shine. The ancient stories of beings who achieved such feats are not tall tales or mythologies, although most on earth believe they are myths because they cannot fathom that a person has absolute power and control over their physical reality.

Only a perfect or near-perfect saint, wizard, or mystic who has absolute faith in the total omnipotency of the God-energy in their heart zone can Paramorph to PRLs where the dead are brought back to life, for example. Only an absolute master, one who is always consciously united with the pure I AM, God, can faithfully embody such a PRL without friction and thus, materialize it. But yes, the answer to this question is that with God, ALL PRLs are possible. All. Not some, not most, not almost everything, but ALL, because God is infinite and you are made in his image. There is nothing stopping you from being a master, but masters choose themselves through the level of faith they exhibit. If you wish to be a Chosen One, you must choose yourself. No one else can.

Earth's physical constraints and density might seem frustrating, but they have their purpose. The seeming solidity of this realm and the relatively slow pace at which objects shift through time and space offer souls the invaluable opportunity to learn patience, persistence, and conviction. In addition, the stiff boundaries and natural laws of the earth, such as mortality, ensure that your experience as a human is richly authentic and feels "truly real", as opposed to just being a simulation or illusion. The human body feels pain, bleeds, and gets tired, but playing the game of life on earth in a human skinsuit is a task that only a master soul would choose. **You, dear reader, are a master soul.** Of course, if you have perfect faith, you can transcend anything, including natural laws, and invoke miracles. Miracles are nothing but your higher God-self changing reality in ways beyond the grasp of your 3D mind.

I find it difficult to conceive that I am actually everything. How can I be everything if everyone else is also everything? If I am infinite, how can others be infinite too? I know the human mind cannot grasp infinite in any meaningful way, but I wonder how there can be "multiple infinities", so to speak. Am I the same as others, or is there any difference between me, a friend, an animal, an insect, and a blade of grass? If all of God exists in every piece of God, aren't we the same?

There is only one infinity, one whole, one unity, one God. This is pure consciousness or I AM. However, each person, animal, plant, and even rock (yes, "inanimate objects" are actually conscious) is a unique point of consciousness or individualized perspective from which this one God sees himself. Suppose you were a vast forest, consisting of plants, animals, insects, and other organisms, and you sought to understand yourself. You could reduce yourself to being a small beetle, and you could get one specific view of the forest in which even blades of grass appear to be massive towers. Alternatively, you could take the form of a deer and view the grass as small and delicious food straws. From the standpoint of a giant tree, you would perceive all animals and insects to be tiny dots moving far below while you are surrounded by the blue sky. Each unique perspective, whether it be insects, animals, or trees, affords you the chance to experientially and richly experience your wholeness, one unique perspective at a time. You could not do this in your original state as the whole forest! This is why God, who is ALL THAT IS, forgets himself and throws on an infinite number of veils or shades to enjoy different experiences and answer the question "Who Am I?".

What is the point of learning to create reality, if all of this is ultimately an illusion? Paramorphing says that I AM, or pure consciousness, is the only objective reality while all PRL templates exist eternally. Spiritual traditions like Sufism, Vedanta, mysticism, and many others speak about self-realization, nirvana, or "enlightenment". Is it right to have desires or pursue them?

Desires are the mechanism through which God explores himself in infinite ways to discover that he is, indeed, God. Each desire has a corresponding PRL, and if you have a burning desire that lights your heart on fire, it is a guarantee that God seeks to experience that portion of his infinite self through you. You are invaluable, in other words, because God needs YOU to find and experience himself. God consists of all PRLs, and all realities were created in a single instant. You never create anything new, because all PRLs were already made and exist as latent potential. This is what Jesus means when he declares "In my father's house there are many mansions". Each person is a point of divine consciousness, a child of God, through which God explores his infinite being by experiencing infinite realities. You determine which room in the infinite divine mansion you experience by who you are conscious of being.

There is nothing wrong with staying in the pure consciousness state of I AM. Many saints and mystics have reached the ecstatic bliss of being absorbed in God's divine I AM, either fully or partially, and the state is absolutely beautiful because there are no cravings there. However, understand that you are NO LESS to any of these saints! You are fundamentally no different from a Krishna, a Jesus, a Rumi, or a Buddha. As stated in the Book of John, "As many as received Him, to them He gave the right to become children of God". You are a Child of God, imbued with infinite power, but what does it mean to "receive him"? Receiving is simply awakening to the power of your inner being, your sense of I AM and the infinite possibilities it contains. You are, in fact, already enlightened so there is no "journey" or "spiritual goal" to achieve. You are already a whole and perfect ray of God who simply consciously decided to forget your divine identity as the whole Creator, so you could enjoy an infinite array of limited experiences in an infinite array of timelines. You are not a mere mortal, but God clothed in flesh! Never forget this.

You can choose to stay in the desireless I AM, dwelling in the bliss of pure consciousness which is the only objective reality. Alternatively, you can realize that you are a boundless Creator God and enjoy yourself by Paramorphing to different PRLs. Experience is a beautiful thing. God in his original state of wholeness, for example, does not know the difference between **giving** love and **receiving** love because he is the giver of love, the receiver of love, and love itself rolled into one composite whole, without separation. When you forget that you are God and become human, you can understand and feel the difference between giving and receiving love, for instance, and countless other experiential permutations that you cannot really experience when you remain the ONE whole.

Neither option is wrong. However, if you decide you would like to experience a new reality or desire, Paramorphing simply offers the metaphysical formula and spiritual science for achieving precisely that.

There is another important consideration. Artificially bypassing your spiritual journey does not work. You might think you are ready to permanently reside in the desireless state of I AM, but if you suppress your inner impulses and desires, they will bubble and boil up inside of you. Do not pretend to be desireless if you are not. Having desires does not lessen you or diminish you in any way. There is nothing wrong, shameful, or inferior about desiring PRLs in which you enjoy fame, wealth, physical pleasures, and any other experiences your heart seeks. Accept the fact that you have these desires, and do not chastise yourself. Seeking to fulfill your desires does not make you weak or unworthy. However, never forget the bigger divine picture: You are not a mortal beggar waiting for the universe to throw you scraps, but the all-powerful Creator, God, temporarily clothed in human form. You are spirit made into flesh, and no desire is greater or more satisfying than the fundamental desire of knowing your truest identity as God himself.

If, at some point, you have had your fill of experiences and are appropriately satiated, you may spontaneously turn inward toward residing in the pure I AM state, realizing that you are always God regardless of whatever PRL you are experiencing. But it must be a natural progression. Do not take shortcuts and pretend that you don't have desires by stifling them. God cannot be fooled, tricked, or deceived in any way. Simply remain honest, and things will unfold perfectly.

You mention that following the heart's Harmonic Signature is absolutely vital to getting everything you want in life. Why is this? Is it really true that by pursuing my truest calling in life, I will get all my desires?

Your heart's Harmonic Signature is your unique variant of God's energy, which is omnipotent, unlimited, eternal, and connected to every single PRL template. Your heart's loving conviction is the energy that transforms a PRL template from a latent possibility that exists in the Eternal Cosmic Library to your experienced physical reality. When you start following your heart's intuitive guidance on what you should spend your time doing, thinking, and dwelling on, you become a supercharged divine magnet that starts attracting everything that you love and desire into your life, rapidly and effortlessly. Think about it this way: What would you spend your time doing if you already had everything you desired? If you had the income and wealth you desired, would you spend time working a job you despised? Of course not. You would spend your time pursuing your heart's calling, whether it be running your own business, snowboarding, recording music albums, day trading, or any number of other activities. You might even choose to continue working at the same job, but with cheer and freedom knowing you are safe no matter what, instead of worrying about being fired or desperately trying to impress your boss or co-workers. Once you embody the state of being in alignment with your heart's harmonic signature, you are effectively announcing and declaring to the universe that you already have everything you could possibly desire. The divine printer, of course, will have no choice but to reflect that back to you and start rapidly Paramorphing you to PRLs in which all your wishes start falling in your lap.

If the heart zone is infinitely powerful, why should we care about the head zone, our limited conscious mind, and the actions we take? Why is the conscious mind even required?

Your heart zone is your tether and link to your omnipotent God-self, but it does not judge, nor does it have preferences around what reality you should experience. Your head zone has no power on its own but is capable of picking and selecting any PRL as your destination. The two must work together. Let us take the analogy of a ship. Your heart zone is the engine of the boat, and your head zone is the steering wheel. A boat with a perfect engine but no steering wheel is functionally useless, as you can't control where you are going, though you have unlimited propulsion power at your disposal. A boat with an excellent steering wheel but no engine is also functionally useless, because you can control where you are going but have no propulsion power to reach your destination. You need both the heart zone, which provides God's infinite power to breathe life into any PRL, and the head zone, which allows you to consciously choose which PRL to embody out of a field of infinite possibilities. When the head and heart work together in seamless harmony, your new PRL is born into physical reality.

I have tried imagining and visualizing my dream reality, using both the inside-out and outside-in methods, but I still feel depressed and anxious about whether my desires will actually come to fruition. My impatience is killing me as I wait for my dreams to come true. What do I do?

Remember one fundamentally vital point: You are NOT imagining and visualizing to create something new or to receive a PRL that is "somewhere out there" in the future. Paramorphing certainly helps you fulfill all your dreams and desires, but the greater story is that ALL DESIRES come from God's desire to know himself as God. You must treat your imagination as REALITY. You are lighting up a PRL that YOU ALREADY HAVE.

If you perform the Paramorphing application techniques from the standpoint of being a small and limited human, you are not invoking your divine identity as a child of God. Therefore, realize that you are not trying to create, manifest, or move to a PRL that is outside of you. Your heart zone is connected to God's Eternal Cosmic Library where all PRLs exist. There is no chance of you failing to move to your dream reality BECAUSE IT LITERALLY ALREADY EXISTS, though you do not see it right now. If you can imagine it, it already exists as a PRL template in God's divine mind. Now, lovingly immerse yourself in your new desired PRL and know that you do not have to struggle. It is already yours.

You must realize that you are not a powerless human being begging for a better life, but the Supreme Creator, God, exploring his infinitude by experiencing new PRLs. When you conceive yourself to be a human, your desires are put on a pedestal, and you doubt whether they can be achieved. When you conceive and truly feel yourself to be God, the eternal consciousness that creates all things, you will automatically feel worthy of any PRL without pedestalizing, fearing, or doubting it. When you are God, all things are feasible, accessible, and subordinate to you. Do not forget this! Paramorphing can get you everything you desire, but the ultimate purpose of the universe and the divine law of Paramorphing is to get you to awaken to your inner Godhood.

What about people who don't know about Paramorphing? Are they creating their worlds and realities in some way, or do they experience events randomly in life?

Nothing, absolutely nothing, is random. When something appears to be random, it simply means that your limited 3D mind has not understood or perceived the subtle Paramorphing Chain of causation that led to it. Each person creates his or her entire experience of reality. However, most people are not aware of this because they do not pay attention. If you do not monitor your attention, you may unconsciously create realities that you do not want. For instance, if you watch enough news programming about financial crises and debts while becoming emotionally charged with fear, anxiety, and anger, you will surely end up materializing a physical reality in which money is hard to come by and those around you bitterly complain about poverty and the unfairness of life. If you change the channel of your attention to desired PRLs, your physical reality will shift correspondingly. Everyone creates their entire reality. **The question, therefore, is not whether you create your reality, but whether you are creating a reality that you truly desire. Paramorphing helps you achieve exactly this.**

I get frustrated when I deal with the things I don't want in the world. Why do opposites exist? Why would God, who is pure love, allow for the possibility of undesirable realities such as pain, suffering, poverty, and illness? I would like to embody my chosen PRLs of health, abundance, and joy, but I really resent the fact that PRLs with the opposite conditions exist.

God is all things, and will always be all things. All, by definition, includes every conceivable PRL. No piece of God can be destroyed. In fact, if you resist and detest PRLs that you deem "undesirable", you crystallize and harden them into physical reality because whatever PRL you place your attention on, with conviction, comes to life. Do not run away from opposites, for what you run away from will only chase you more rapidly. Simply look at the PRL you do not want, boldly and bravely, and accept that it has a RIGHT to exist in God's Eternal Cosmic Library. All things have a right to exist as templates in God's mind. Once you have accepted and surrendered to the fact that realities you do not desire also have a right to exist, you will find that their grasp on you slowly starts to diminish! Realize that PRLs that you find "undesirable" or "contrary" to your wishes are to be appreciated, for these opposites are needed to show you what you DO want. The value of abundance and wealth can only be seen when paired against the opposite condition of poverty. The beauty of light can only be fully appreciated against the contrast of darkness. Do not run away from PRLs that you don't want. Accept and appreciate their place in the eternal cosmic order, without fighting them, then turn your attention lovingly and with conviction to the PRLs that you do wish to embody. Then, your desired PRLs will come to life and the undesired PRLs will vanish.

Many people ask the universe for signs or early hints that their wishes are coming true. Are there any reliable external indicators that our desired PRLs are crystallizing into physical reality?

The world can only reflect who you are conscious of being. The physical reality you observe outside of you all comes from within you! You are the sole creative power that directs your entire life experience. This means that signs, indicators, and synchronicities come from within you. For example, suppose you wish to have a cherry red Jeep. You use the Paramorphing techniques to embody the PRL in which you already have the vehicle, and spontaneously and naturally feel a sense of warmth, joy, and gratitude for being given your desire. A few days later, you might notice a neighbor's kid who unexpectedly brings you a toy red Jeep from his playing car collection. Or, a family member who has never been fond of Jeeps might suddenly make a remark expressing favorability toward Jeeps! The beauty of signs and synchronicities is that others might find them to be banal or coincidental, but to YOU, they will be unmistakable proof and precursors of your new desired PRL. Of course, know that the signs and synchronicities are not outside of you, but simple second-order effects of your firm conviction to occupy and embody your new PRL. The best sign or synchronicity of all is your unwavering internal conviction that you are ALREADY in your new desired PRL, no matter what physical circumstances you may be experiencing now. When you see a sign or synchronicity, simply relax and know that your new PRL is unfolding smoothly, perfectly, and harmoniously, and simply give thanks for it. It is already yours.

Can I visit other realms with Paramorphing? Where do I go when I dream? Sometimes I feel like my entire life is a dream.

Every realm, life, experience, and plane of existence exists here and now. In any given lifetime, you are merely focusing on one version of yourself that exists as a specific lifeform (such as a human being), on a specific planet, in a specific universe, in a specific time period, and with a specific set of characteristics. However, in reality, you are all objects, creatures, and experiences across every possible variant of time and space. You chose to forget that you are the WHOLE so you could have a realistic experience of one particular life. When you dream, your consciousness floats to various other PRLs. You may experience another PRL in full, or experience bits and pieces of other PRLs mashed together, but the key point to remember is that dreams are not merely delusions or random spurts of brain activity. They are episodes in which you travel to other PRLs because when you sleep, your conscious, rational mind (the head zone) shuts off and descends into the heart, where all PRLs in God's Eternal Cosmic Library exist.

Nightmares or dreams with undesirable experiences are a

function of thoughts and emotions that you may have repressed or battled with while you were awake. Nightmares are a blessing, in a sense, for they allow you to process these emotions through a painful dream experience as opposed to a painful experience in physical reality. Of course, your physical reality is as much a dream as your dreams at night, but most people would prefer to process trauma through their dreams at night rather than via their physical reality while awake. Negative dreams are not a harbinger of bad things to come. They are psychic pressure valves that allow you to vent emotional steam so that you can be happier and more peaceful when you are awake. For example, suppose you visit a zoo. Your mind might be filled with repressed fear and anxiety about snakebites after visiting the snake exhibit, so you might experience a nightmare in which a python chases you through a forest. However, this is preferable to carrying around the fear while awake; if you continue to fearfully dwell on snakes while you are awake, you may crystallize a physical PRL in which you do suffer a snakebite! Nightmares are gifts from the creator that enable us to process and dilute burdensome emotions and states of mind without drawing them into our physical reality.

Fortuitous dreams with desirable events and experiences, on the other hand, are often signs of good fortune to come. If you have mentally and imaginatively embodied a new PRL with a certain desire, and you dream of that desire, this is a near-certain indication that the desire is yours and is rapidly unfolding into physical reality. It is not necessary to have a dream to materialize a PRL, of course, but a vivid dream involving the realization of your desire is a near-perfect guarantee that your new PRL is rapidly taking shape. In many cases, people have such vivid dreams that they palpably feel themselves as having received their desire. When they wake up, they don't see their new PRL yet, but their dream is so incredibly compelling, vivid, and realistic that they somehow know, with deep conviction, that their desire will show up in their physical reality. In other words, they truly feel that they already HAVE their desire, no matter what their current physical reality shows. And of course, when a person has such an unrelenting conviction in a new PRL, regardless of what their present circumstances may be, that new reality invariably crystallizes and comes to life. This is why dreams are so powerful.

If all PRLs come from ONE God or Source, why does each have a different energetic signature or "feel"? How can something that was ONE truly become MANY?

God or Source is the only reality that underlies ALL things. However, God forgets himself to experience himself in an infinite number of ways. If each PRL had the same energetic feel, God would have no variety and be incapable of richly and authentically experiencing himself in different ways. However, it is important to note that God remains at the core of ALL PRLs. Each PRL, in other words, consists of the ONE energy of God, pure creation love, covered by different shades or filters that create an infinite number of possible experiences. God, however, remains unchanged deep down no matter what shades or filters are placed on top of him.

However, it is clear that some PRLs are preferable to others. Almost all people desire health, abundance, joy, vibrancy, creativity, and love. God, or pure Source, is perfect health, eternal life, infinite, ceaseless abundance, unlimited joy, and the highest degree of love. The PRLs that people typically desire are really just PRLs that are closest to God. God is present in all PRLs, but PRLs differ in the depth and intensity of the filters/shades they place on top of this pure Source energy. A PRL of health, joy, and love has a very thin filter of obfuscating energy that covers up the Source because God himself is eternal life, perfect health, ceaseless creative joy, boundless cosmic power, and sublime love. On the other hand, a PRL of disease, pessimism, hate, and cynicism requires a very thick filter of obfuscating energy on top of Source. God can never be destroyed even in the most distressing PRLs, but his presence can be temporarily forgotten or only dimly felt when a person experiences these realities.

Think of God, the infinitely loving Source, as an infinitely pure and bright light without any lampshades covering it. When this pure light wishes to experience itself by asking the question "Who Am I?", an infinite number of lampshades were created, each altering the pure light of Source in a unique way and creating a unique variant of light. However, at the core, God is unchanged no matter what temporary lampshade is placed over him. Lampshades represent PRLs. PRLs with health, love, joy, vitality, and abundance can be thought of as thin, almost transparent lampshades that allow the light of God to shine with minimal obfuscation. PRLs with misery, hate, sickness, and poverty can be thought of as dark, thick lampshades that heavily mute and stifle God's light.

In the end, though, no PRL is good or bad. To God, they are all merely experiences. You, however, as an individualized son or daughter of God, can choose which PRL you would like to embody. So, simply define your own PRL identity without judging other PRLs as inferior or unworthy. Once you do this, your outer world will most certainly shift to reflect the PRL you identify as.

This all makes perfect sense now, but even after realizing I am a son or daughter of God, I still have a particular fondness and sense of reverential love toward saints and masters like Jesus and Krishna. I have also heard many masters telling their followers to simply trust and follow me and you will be taken care of. Can you please provide some guidance?

Saints, masters, and mystics like Jesus are very real, but they are not authority figures that demand or mandate your love. They are the epitome of divine love, compassion, and free will. Jesus Christ is not some stern authoritarian, but your divine elder brother who realized his oneness with the Father, Source, and came to share this message with the world. Krishna was the same. When Krishna assumed his universal form, or Vishwaroopam, he taught the charioteer Arjuna that man is not a small and limited being but infinite God temporarily assuming a human form. Krishna's Bhagavad Gita awoke Arjuna to the infinite possibilities that lay nested within him as a Son of God. The great spiritual masters did not come to Earth to lord over you as authority figures. Rather, they assumed human forms to awaken you to the fact that we are all brothers of the ONE father, I AM. Belief and conviction alone create your reality, so even if you do not have perfect conviction in yourself, for instance, you may have a perfect sense of conviction in Jesus, and that will cause your desired PRLs to crystallize into solid reality. Alternatively, you may have perfect faith that visiting a saint's tomb or healing spring can cure your illness, and if your belief is pure, you most certainly will be healed. There is nothing wrong with choosing an external saint, mystic, or other spiritual figure as your teacher or the bedrock on which your faith rests. In some cases, people might feel a deep connection to spiritual figures such as guardian angels or representatives of their higher selves who awaken them to their heart's harmonic signature and what their truest and greatest purpose on earth is. Sometimes, people in NDEs (near-death experiences) experience the beautiful astral planes of heaven and come face-to-face with Jesus and God in the form of blindingly beautiful light, love, and peace. All these are wonderful things, indeed. Just don't forget that underneath it all, you, the angels, Jesus, Krishna, and all things in the cosmos are waves of ONE divine ocean, GOD. And you, as a child of God, have a right to ALL of it! What you truly believe creates your entire reality.

We will conclude with one simple, powerful, and succinct teaching from Jesus that beautifully summarizes Paramorphing: **"Therefore I tell you, whatever you ask for in prayer, believe that you have received it, and it will be yours"**.

L'alam al-mein. Aa-meen.

www.ingramcontent.com/pod-product-compliance
Lightning Source LLC
Chambersburg PA
CBHW070952180426
43194CB00042B/2360